I0797822

The Happy Bonsai Handbook

First published in Great Britain in 2025
by Mitchell Beazley, an imprint of Octopus
Publishing Group Ltd, Carmelite House,
50 Victoria Embankment, London EC4Y 0DZ
www.octopusbooks.co.uk
www.octopusbooksusa.com

An Hachette UK Company
www.hachette.co.uk

The authorized representative in the EEA is Hachette Ireland,
8 Castlecourt Centre, Dublin 15, D15 XTP3, Ireland
(email: info@hbgi.ie)

ISBN: 9781840919912
eISBN: 9781840919929

A CIP record of this book is available from the British Library
Set in Mamut/Cantoria created by Josse Pickard
Printed and bound in Huizhou, Guangdong, China
TT/Jul/2025
10 9 8 7 6 5 4 3 2 1

Conceived, designed and produced by
The Bright Press, an imprint of the Quarto Group,
1 Triptych Place, London SE1 9SH
www.quarto.com

Publisher	James Evans
Editorial Director	Isheeta Mustafi
Art Director	Emily Nazer
Managing Editor	Lucy Tipton
Publishing Operations Director	Kathy Turtle
Production Controller	George Li
Editor	Nick Pierce
Project Editor	Julie Brooke
Design	JC Lanaway
Publishing Assistant	Jemima Solley
Picture Research	Charlotte Rivers
Illustrations	Sarah Skeate
Cover Design	Marcia Pedraza
Consultant	Bjorn Bjorholm

Publisher for Mitchell Beazley: Alison Starling
Assistant Editor for Mitchell Beazley: Ellen Sleath

Front cover: Shutterstock/Mario Savoia
Back cover: Shutterstock/PrimeMockup

The Happy Bonsai Handbook

ADAM McCALLION

MITCHELL BEAZLEY

Contents

Foreword

Bonsai is a unique art form, as the medium we work with is living plant material that is forever growing, shifting and elongating.

A work of bonsai art is never static, but always changing with the seasons. Each time a bonsai is styled then restyled by subsequent artists, that tree becomes a snapshot of the artist's perception of nature in that given moment.

Much of what we do in bonsai design is dictated by the plant itself – whether that be defoliation to create branch ramification, pruning shoots to develop bifurcations in the structure or replenishing the soil as the tree becomes root-bound over time. What may seem to be simple horticultural practice to the uninitiated is the basis for creating bonsai art over many years or decades.

I have always taken the view that bonsai is an 'emergent art' – the beauty and aesthetic qualities that we seek to create in a tree emerge over time as a result of applying repeated horticultural practices. While the thought of investing years in a single tree to develop it as a bonsai might deter some from even attempting the hobby, for those who stick with it the rewards are well worth the investment.

This brings me to the subject of this excellent new bonsai book. Adam has managed to take many of these seemingly daunting subjects surrounding bonsai art and has deftly condensed the information into a fun, easily digestible format. *The Happy Bonsai Handbook* is exactly that – an enjoyable read through the most up-to-date bonsai techniques currently being utilized by bonsai practitioners from around the world. This is certainly the type of book I wish was available when I began my bonsai journey so many decades ago at the age of 13!

BJORN L BJORHOLM
Eisei-en Kyoto
www.eisei-en.com

Opposite: The weathered deadwood of this twin-trunk Chinese juniper 'Itoigawa' (*Juniperus chinensis* 'itoigawa') is a testament to the passage of time.

Introduction

Welcome to *The Happy Bonsai Handbook*! This book is a fun and practical guide for anyone looking to get started with bonsai or take their trees to the next level.

I'm Adam McCallion, a bonsai artist from Derry, Northern Ireland. I started my bonsai journey in 2019 and have spent the years since learning everything I can about bonsai, from working with top artists across the world to experimenting with my own trees at home. I now teach bonsai through workshops and online videos across YouTube, Instagram, TikTok and Facebook, where I've connected with thousands of other bonsai enthusiasts.

My goal is simple: to make bonsai easy to understand, enjoyable to learn and accessible to everyone! Maybe you have received your first tree as a gift, or you just want to try your hand at this wonderful hobby… Whatever the reason, this book will guide you step by step through the essential techniques and bonsai care tips you need to grow healthy, thriving bonsai with confidence.

Right: A mature hinoki cypress (*Chamaecyparis obtusa*) bonsai with a good branch structure and the start of good ramification. Although this tree looks amazing, it could be refined further over another five years.

Bonsai basics

Discover the basics of bonsai care, the tools you will need and some great species that, as a beginner, you can work with. You will also find a directory of bonsai styles, tips for how to avoid common mistakes and advice on starting your bonsai journey with the right mindset.

Welcome to the world of bonsai

When translated from Japanese, the term bonsai means 'planted in a pot' or, more accurately, 'planted in a container'. In kanji, 'bon' or 盆 means 'tray', and 'sai' or 栽 means 'plant' or 'planting'. However, anyone who practises the art of bonsai knows that a lot more goes in to bonsai than just putting any old tree in a pot.

WHAT IS A BONSAI?

Any species of tree can be made into a bonsai. This is because the term bonsai does not necessarily refer to the tree itself, but the practice of pruning and shaping it over many years to keep it small. Bonsai is about working with a tree's natural characteristics and using these traits to create a miniature, accurate representation of a larger tree than would be found in the wild. It is about creating an artistic expression that tells a story and evokes an emotional response from the viewer. The movement of the trunk and branches, the texture and colour of the bark, the planting angle and how much deadwood and visible age there are all add to the visual narrative.

When I first got started in bonsai, I used to think that a bonsai was a genetically modified tree that naturally grew small. I even ended up falling for the classic scam of buying 'bonsai seeds' hoping to grow a beautiful maple bonsai with vibrant blue leaves. When the seeds came of course they didn't grow. There is no such thing as a bonsai seed, and there are certainly no maples with leaves as blue as the sky as I had been promised.

Opposite: This Japanese white pine (*Pinus parviflora*) has been developed into a superb bonsai.

Choosing the right tree: bonsai species for beginners

For the beginner, the huge number of bonsai species can be overwhelming. I recommend choosing a tree that you like the look of, one that is easy to care for, fast growing and suitable for your local climate.

STARTER TREES

Like me, your first bonsai may be given to you as a gift, or you may have seen some in the houseplant section of a garden centre or a big-box store and thought, 'Why not pick one up and give it a go?' Starting your bonsai adventure with such a tree is a brilliant way to get into the hobby. It allows you to begin with a tree that already looks presentable, which can be a confidence-booster as you take care of it. Many of these starter bonsai are quite forgiving, with qualities that make them perfect for beginners. The type of tree that suits you best will depend on whether you would prefer for your bonsai to live indoors or outdoors.

There are many ways to start your first bonsai. You can grow one from seed (see page 142), take cuttings (see page 150) or even create a new tree through air layering (see page 154). Giving a tree its first repot (see page 126) or styling (see page 162) are great ways to start using bonsai techniques.

Specialized species

If you would like to begin with a more specialized species, such as a Japanese white pine (*Pinus parviflora*), Deshōjō Maple (*Acer palmatum* 'Deshōjō'), or Satsuki Azalea (*Rhododendron indicum*) I recommend buying a starter tree from a bonsai nursery.

BONSAI CLASSIFICATION

Bonsai are usually thought of as 'small trees', but they come in many different sizes. Bonsai are traditionally classified into one of ten groups relative to their scale. Each size brings its own care needs, styling challenges and even different ways to display the tree at exhibitions.

Keshitsubo
3–7.5cm (1–3in.)

Shito
7.5cm (3in.)

Mame
5–15cm (2–6in)

Shohin
12–20cm (5–8in)

Komono
15–25cm (6–10in)

Katade-mochi
25–45cm (10–18in)

Chumono/Chiu
40–90cm (16–36in)

Omono/Da
75–120cm (30–48in)

Hachi-uye
100–150cm (40–60in)

Imperial
150–200cm (60–80in)

Ficus

Ficus is a great choice for beginners who want to grow an indoor bonsai. Varieties such as *Ficus benjamina*, *Ficus microcarpa* and *Ficus retusa* handle low light and low humidity well, which is normal for indoor environments. They may not thrive right away, but they will survive while you learn about and improve your bonsai care. *Ficus* often drop their leaves when moved to new environments, but will soon produce a new crop of growth.

Chinese Elm

The Chinese Elm (*Ulmus parvifolia*) is one of the most popular outdoor bonsai species. Some sellers classify this species as an indoor and outdoor tree. Although it is possible, it can be tricky to grow indoors. Personally, I class it as an outdoor tree simply because it is much easier to care for outdoors. It is relatively forgiving when slightly under- or overwatered, but it is prone to root rot if the soil does not drain well.

Cotoneaster

The cotoneaster has beautiful small leaves and berries that make it highly suitable for bonsai. It is good for beginners because it grows fast and responds extremely well to pruning by sending out lots of back-buds. It can tolerate soil that has dried out a little, but for a happy tree remember to keep on top of the watering.

Japanese larch

The Japanese larch (*Larix kaempferi*) is one of my favourite beginner-friendly trees. It is easy to train and grows incredibly quickly, allowing you to achieve a presentable bonsai in less time. Its delicate, needle-like foliage grows in a compact, refined manner. This tree prefers consistently moist soil, so be sure to keep up with watering it.

Tools of the trade: what you need to get started

Initially, I was put off by the number of specialist tools I thought I needed to get started in bonsai. But you can easily manage with an ordinary pair of garden scissors or secateurs – just make sure that they are clean and sharp.

As you get more into growing bonsai, you can slowly expand your tool collection to suit your needs. Having access to bonsai tools makes certain cuts a lot easier and faster. You can only cut a branch so close to a trunk with garden scissors and secateurs before you need to switch to branch cutters for a more flush cut (a cut level with the trunk or branch).

Opposite: Add new items to your toolbox as your skills and trees develop so that you can build on the equipment available to you. Shown here is a young Chinese Elm (*Ulmus parvifolia*), a forgiving species ideal for beginners. You can see how a pair of branch cutters can help you achieve closer cuts.

BASIC BONSAI TOOLS

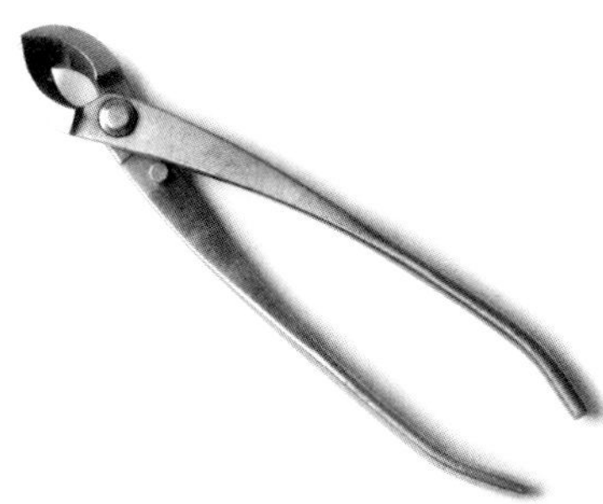

Concave branch cutters

This tool is used to make clean, precise cuts on thicker branches around 1–2cm (½–¾in) thick. Concave branch cutters allow you to cut branches closer to the trunk. They take a concave bite out of the tree which helps the wound to callus flush with the trunk instead of bulging out as with a flat cut.

Root-pruning shears

These are designed for pruning the tree roots. The wider handles provide a better grip, and the thicker blades can withstand slicing through soil and the occasional stubborn root.

Twig cutters

Sometimes referred to as Satsuki shears, twig cutters are long-handled scissors designed for pruning thin branches 5–7mm (¼in) thick. They are used for detailed pruning because the long handles help you get into tight spaces in the canopy.

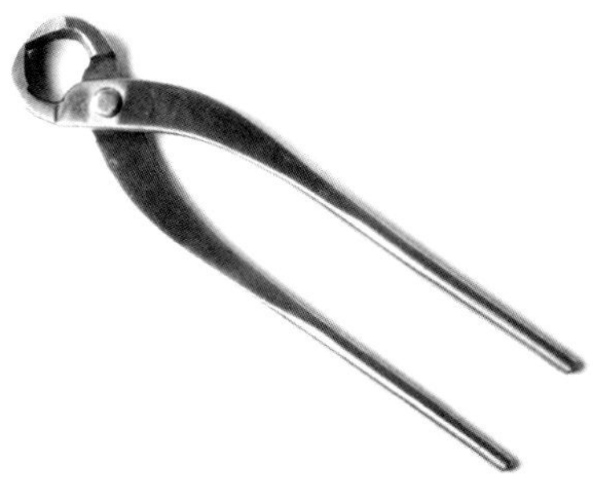

Root cutters

These are used on thicker roots which cannot be cut with root-pruning shears. Their strong, sharp blades are flat where they meet which allows you to achieve precise, clean cuts that promote better healing. This tool is suited to cut roots that are 2–3cm (¾–1¼in) thick.

Jin pliers

If you would like to create deadwood features such as *jin* and *shari* (see page 175) you need a pair of *jin* pliers. The fine teeth of the gripping section allow you to crush, grip and strip the bark off a branch. They are also invaluable when wiring the ends of branches and wiring trees into a pot.

Wire cutters

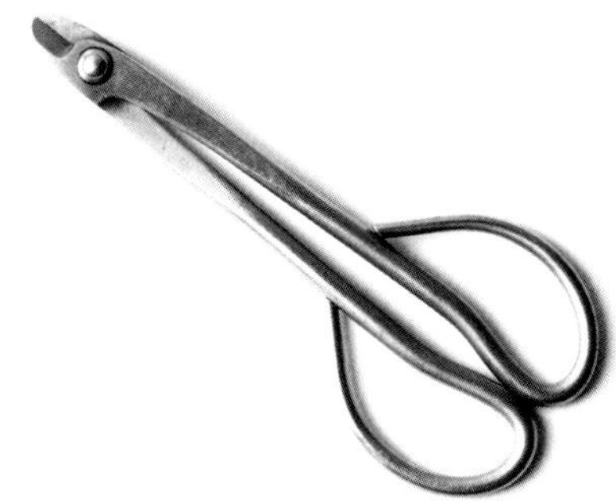

Excellent for cutting aluminium or copper wire, these are also essential when removing wire from branches that have set in place. Their rounded edges give you more precise cuts that ensure the wire is cut cleanly without biting into the bark of your tree.

Root rake

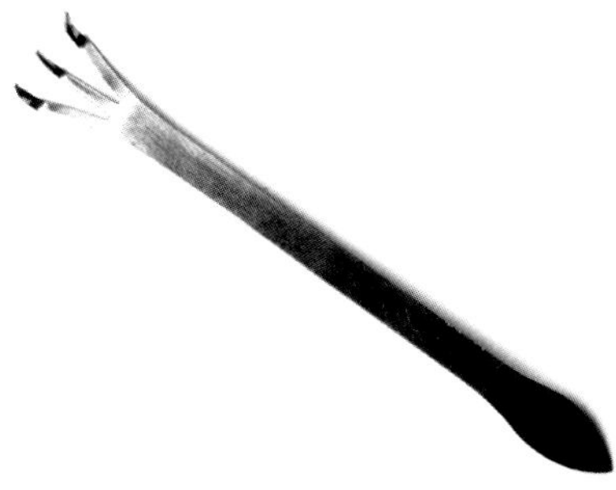

This is used during repotting to carefully loosen the old soil and untangle the roots with minimal damage. Of course, if you do not have a root rake, you can do what I did when I was getting started and bend the prongs of a table fork. I still sometimes use my homemade root rake today.

Bonsai styles: finding your tree's personality

The many different styles and sizes of bonsai have been given names to make them easy to categorise. However, these should only serve as a general guideline when creating a tree. Every tree is different, and they may not all conform to these types.

When it comes to creating a tree, following the style of traditional Japanese bonsai styles is a great place to start as they give a general guide to follow. They are inspired by how trees grow in the wild, whether they have been twisted by the wind, weighed down by snow, or even when they are reaching for the sun on the side of a cliff. These styles will help you to understand how to build structure and movement and from that point start to experiment with your own style.

Keep it natural

When styling a tree, work with its natural shape and movement, rather than forcing it into a style that doesn't suit it.

Opposite: This large ficus (*Ficus retusa*) has been kept in a humid environment which has encouraged it to send out lots of aerial roots.

Formal upright (*chokkan*)

This is the classic bonsai style with a vertical straight trunk that tapers from the base to the apex with a balanced branch placement.

Species to try: Japanese black pine (*Pinus thunbergii*), Japanese larch (*Larix kaempferi*), white spruce (*Picea glauca*) and Dawn redwood (*Metasequoia glyptostroboides*).

Informal upright (*moyogi*)

Also known as an S-curve bonsai, it has a flowing nature with gentle bends in the trunk. Branches come from the outside of each bend, similar to trees in nature.

Species to try: Japanese maple (*Acer palmatum*), Chinese juniper (*Juniperus chinensis*), ficus (*Ficus microcarpa*) and Chinese elm (*Ulmus parvifolia*).

Twin trunk (*sōkan*)

Here, two trunks grow from a single root base. One is usually taller than the other, but this is not always the case.

Species to try: Japanese maple (*Acer palmatum*), bald cypress (*Taxodium distichum*), Scots pine (*Pinus sylvestris*) and Ezo spruce (*Picea jezoensis*).

Split trunk (*sabamiki*)

A single tree with a hollow or split down the middle. This style has a lot of character and represents the survival of a tree through harsh conditions.

Species to try: Japanese yew (*Taxus cuspidata*), sargent juniper (*Juniperus chinensis var. sargentii*) and cork bark elm (*Ulmus parvifolia var. corticosa*).

Multi-trunk/clump style (*kabudachi*)

Three or more trunks growing together to form a small cluster of trees. Each trunk may vary in height and thickness so that the tree resembles a forest.

Species to try: Japanese maple (*Acer palmatum*), silver birch (*Betula pendula*), trident maple (*Acer buergerianum*) and ficus (*Ficus benjamina*).

Forest planting (*yose-ue*)

A group of trees planted together to simulate a miniature forest. The trunks can vary in height, thickness and spacing.

Species to try: European hornbeam (*Carpinus betulus*), Japanese zelkova (*Zelkova serrata*), bald cypress (*Taxodium distichum*), European larch (*Larix decidua*) and Amur maple (*Acer tataricum* subsp. *ginnala*).

Cascade (*kengai*) and semi-cascade (*han-kengai*)

The trunk of this tree grows down the side of a tall pot as if it is flowing downwards. The trunk of a cascade extends below the base of the pot; that of a semi-cascade does not fall below it.

Species to try: Western juniper (*Juniperus occidentalis*), Japanese wisteria (*Wisteria floribunda*), bougainvillea (*Bougainvillea glabra*) and white spruce (*Picea glauca*).

Raft (*ikadabuki*)

A single trunk placed on its side with multiple branches growing upwards like individual trees.

Species to try: Japanese quince (*Chaenomeles japonica*), Chinese elm *(Ulmus parvifolia*), trident maple (*Acer buergerianum*) and ficus (*Ficus salicaria*).

Windswept (*fukinagashi*)

All branches and the trunk of the tree flow in one direction as if the tree has been shaped by wind over many years.

Species to try: Scots pine (*Pinus sylvestris*), European beech (*Fagus sylvatica*), sargent juniper (*Juniperus chinensis var. sargentii*) and buttonwood (*Conocarpus erectus*).

Slanted (*shakan*)

The trunk leans to one side with even branch placement. It shows a tree that may slant due to the wind or uneven ground.

Species to try: Japanese black pine (*Pinus thunbergii*), trident maple (*Acer buergerianum*), Chinese hackberry (*Celtis sinensis*) and olive (*Olea europaea*).

Root-over-rock (*seki-jōju*)

A tree with roots growing tightly over and around a rock. This represents trees grown on a craggy terrain, such as mountains, where the roots are forced to search for water in the cracks between rocks.

Species to try: Japanese white pine (*Pinus parviflora*), ficus (*Ficus microcarpa* or *Ficus microcarpa var. crassifolia*) and Japanese maple.

Planted-on-rock (*ishitsuki*)

A tree that has been planted into the crevices of a rock, mimicking trees that hang off rock cliffs.

Species to try: Sargent juniper (*Juniperus chinensis var. sargentii*), Japanese holly (*Ilex crenata*), Japanese quince (*Chaenomeles japonica*) and shore juniper (*Juniperus rigida*).

Broom (*hokidachi*)

A straight upright trunk with branches coming from all directions at a single point at the top so that it resembles a broom.

Species to try: Japanese zelkova (*Zelkova serrata*), Chinese elm (*Ulmus parvifolia*), maidenhair tree (*Ginkgo biloba*) and field maple (*Acer campestre*).

Exposed root (*neagari*)

The roots that support the tree extend above the soil before merging into the trunk.

Species to try: Brazilian rain tree (*Pithecellobium tortum*), ficus (*Ficus microcarpa* 'Tiger Bark'), Japanese black pine (*Pinus thunbergii*) and trident maple (*Acer buergerianum*).

Literati (*bunjin*)

This delicate form is tall and slender and features sparse branches at the apex.

Species to try: Japanese red pine (*Pinus densiflora*), Japanese black pine (*Pinus thunbergii*), eastern white cedar (*Thuja occidentalis*), shore juniper (*Juniperus rigida*) and tamarisk (*Tamarix spp.*).

Beginner blunders: learning from your mistakes

Opposite: Indoor sweet plum (*Sageretia theezans*) are sold as starter trees. But this species can be sensitive to changes in its environment, so consistent care is key.

Below: As the health of my first bonsai – an indoor sweet plum – began to decline the top started to die first, followed by the base of the tree.

Even the most experienced bonsai artists can get things wrong and sometimes lose a tree. This is okay. What truly matters in life is learning from our errors and improving, making them less likely to happen again.

On my 21st birthday, my partner Daryl gifted me my very first bonsai, an indoor sweet plum (*Sageretia theezans*). This tree had great sentimental value to me because it was a gift from him, and I wanted to do everything I could to keep it alive. I followed every instruction that came with the tree to the letter, including watering it once a week.

GETTING IT RIGHT

Little did I know, this was not the best approach. Everyone's home is different and factors such as humidity and indoor temperatures play crucial roles in keeping your tree alive. Within just one month, I noticed the leaves began to dry up and fall off, and the tree's overall health worsened. By the end of the year, it was, sadly, dead. I was left with so many questions: What went wrong? Could I have prevented this? Do bonsai just die naturally over time?

If you are a beginner and a tree dies on you, do not get discouraged. This is all part of the learning journey which I am also still on myself. Trees sometimes die and when this happens it is a valuable learning experience.

The bonsai mindset: why consistency is key

I believe that a good mindset is crucial for achieving any goal in life, and bonsai is no exception. To care for and develop a tree properly it is vital that you understand the techniques used and always ask yourself why you are doing something.

As you deepen your knowledge of bonsai and understand why you are doing things, you will reduce the risk of losing a tree. Above all, the health of a tree comes first, and this means giving it the best care you can, even if this means it looks unpresentable for a while. Respected bonsai nurseries often have trees that appear unkempt and out of shape while they are given the time to rejuvenate naturally.

LEARNING LESSONS

With bonsai, a good mindset is about having patience, working with your tree and appreciating what it gives to you. It is a long-term commitment that can span many years and requires a good routine. You will face many challenges; I like to see each of them as a lesson. There can be unforeseen weather changes such as a storm, or pests and diseases may attack your tree. A strong outlook and the willingness to adapt and grow transforms a beginner hobbyist into a true artist. This approach can also extend to other areas of your life, teaching you patience, discipline and mindfulness. In many ways, the bonsai can shape you, just as much as you shape the bonsai.

Opposite: This mature Japanese black pine (*Pinus thunbergii*) is a beautiful example of how these trees develop craggy bark when they are more mature.

Where should your bonsai live?

Learn how environmental factors such as lighting, temperature, humidity and airflow can contribute to a healthy tree, and whether they prefer to live indoors or outdoors. Plus find out how to protect your trees when temperatures drop in winter.

The power of placement: how environment shapes your tree

Just like people, trees need the right environment to grow and thrive. Where you place them affects their health and shapes their growth, strength and how long they will live. Understanding four important factors – light, temperature, humidity and airflow – will allow you to create the perfect environment for your tree.

LIGHT

Providing the right amount of light is essential for healthy growing trees. They need light to photosynthesize efficiently, to convert sunlight into the energy that fuels their development. Without sufficient light your tree will not die right away, but over time its leaves will start to drop, growth will slow, and the plant will gradually weaken.

Too much direct sunlight can also be harmful, and some species are more sensitive to overexposure than others. Japanese maples (*Acer palmatum*), for example, can easily get leaf scorch in summer during the hot midday sun, while species such as junipers and pines thrive in full sun. If there is too much sun on a particular day, move your more sensitive trees to a shaded spot or place them under some shade netting.

Opposite: This particular ficus (*Ficus benjamina* 'Natasja') is sometimes referred to as the weeping ficus because its leaves tend to weep downwards. They are fast-growing and thrive in direct sunlight.

Below: Japanese maple (*Acer palmatum*) bonsai in peak autumn colour, accompanied by a Korean hornbeam (*Carpinus turczaninowii*) on the left. These deciduous species thrive outdoors with full sun in spring and autumn, though they benefit from some protection during the summer.

Light requirements vary throughout the year. In spring, when light intensity is still relatively low, it's best to give trees as much direct sunlight as possible (including species such as Japanese maple). In contrast, in winter when most plants are dormant, light requirements become minimal. In fact, all deciduous trees can receive no sunlight all winter without any harm as they lose their leaves and do not photosynthesize at this time. As temperatures rise and daylight length increases after the winter solstice, plants begin to wake up. The opposite occurs following the summer solstice: as daylight hours shorten and temperatures drop, trees become dormant.

TEMPERATURE

Temperature also plays an important role when it comes to the health of your tree. Different species have different requirements. Tropical species prefer warmer conditions while temperate species do best when they experience the changes of the seasons, especially the coldness of winter so that they can enter dormancy.

HUMIDITY

Humidity is particularly important for tropical species such as Fukien tea *(Carmona retusa)*. Dry air can cause the leaves of these indoor species to dry out and drop off. To boost humidity levels in your home, mist the foliage with water or place the tree among other plants. However, too much humidity can cause unwanted fungal problems so be mindful and always check the leaves and surface soil for signs of fungus. Outdoors, natural humidity levels are usually sufficient, but on particularly dry days mist your trees with water or foliar feed when temperatures are lower in the morning or evening and place them in a shaded spot.

AIRFLOW

Good airflow prevents fungal infections, reduces the chances of pests and strengthens the tree. Indoor trees benefit from being placed by an open window with gentle airflow and constant temperature. Alternatively, if the air seems stagnant, position a small electric fan nearby. Make sure outdoor trees are not placed too close together and avoid putting them in the corner of a garden that has poor airflow since this can lead to mould and weak growth.

Changes in temperature

If you are placing your bonsai indoors, avoid positioning it by a radiator as excess heat can dry out the soil and foliage too quickly. Also take care near drafty windows because sudden temperature and humidity fluctuations can be harmful.

Indoors or outdoors? Picking the perfect spot

Choosing the right spot for your bonsai may seem tricky, but it is quite simple once you understand the needs of your trees. Some thrive indoors with stable conditions, while others need to experience the changing seasons outdoors.

INDOOR TREES

Tropical and subtropical species such as the sweet plum (*Sageretia theezans*) and Brazilian rain tree (*Pithecellobium tortum*) can adapt well to indoor conditions. Even though winter temperatures outdoors can kill these trees, they benefit greatly from the occasional outdoor spell during the summer when it is warm enough to give them some real sunlight. When placing your bonsai indoors, aim for a well-lit spot with stable humidity and temperature. Many indoor species can experience leaf drop and other issues if frequently moved or exposed to environmental changes. A south-facing window is ideal, providing plenty of light without direct sun exposure. Avoid placing your bonsai too close to the glass, since temperatures near the window fluctuate, becoming too hot during the day and too cold at night, and this can stress your tree.

All trees are outdoor trees

There is no such thing as an indoor bonsai. In temperate climates, many indoor trees are tropical evergreen species from warmer regions that do not become dormant in winter. In their natural climates, they are simply outdoor trees.

OUTDOOR TREES

Temperate species such as junipers, pines and maples thrive in outdoor environments where they can get fresh air, sunlight and experience seasonal changes. They rely on the natural cycle of the seasons, especially in winter when they become dormant. Without these seasonal changes, their growth will diminish, become more susceptible to pests and diseases and may eventually die. Outdoor bonsai should be placed where they get at least six to eight hours of sunlight per day. Some trees are frost-tolerant, but others need winter protection (see page 48).

Remember – every tree is different, so it is important to research its species if you are unsure of what it needs.

Below left: Place trees that require a lot of sunlight beside a window.

Below right: Rotate bonsai such as this hinoki cypress (*Chamaecyparis obtusa*) regularly so that they receive the same amount of sun all around and do not grow to be one-sided.

Indoor grow lights

When your indoor environment does not have enough light, grow lights are a reliable solution. It is essential to use the right type and intensity of light and place them in the correct position to ensure your trees get the energy they need to grow their best.

TYPES OF GROW LIGHT

It is simply not realistic to hope that the regular lights in your home will be enough for your bonsai. You can buy special bulbs designed for growing plants. Full-spectrum LED or fluorescent lights are the best choices because they are very close to natural sunlight. Chlorophyll, the molecule in plants responsible for converting light into energy (through photosynthesis), mostly absorbs the blue- and red-light spectrums. A well-balanced LED bulb will offer blue light for compact growth and strong foliage and red light to help with branch development and overall tree health. I prefer LED bulbs because they are more energy efficient and produce less heat. Fluorescent T5 and T8 bulbs are also a good option and distribute the light well. Look for a light intensity of 2000–5000 lumens per square foot – use a light meter to test this.

USING GROW LIGHTS

Higher-intensity lights should be placed further away from your trees to prevent the leaves burning, while lower-intensity bulbs can be placed closer to them. For small- to medium-sized trees, a 30W full-spectrum LED placed 15–30cm (6–12in) above a tree is usually sufficient. If you have more than a few trees – or even larger trees – you may need a 50–100W bulb to ensure even coverage. Alternatively, use more than one bulb to cover a few trees at a time.

Opposite:
Professional bonsai growers often use tents fitted with grow lights as their reflective walls allow the light to hit the trees on all sides and can help to maintain a consistent temperature.

Five indoor bonsai for sunny spots

Not every tree likes to be kept in your home, but there are some species that thrive in these conditions if they get plenty of light as well as stable temperatures and humidity levels. Always research the specific needs of your trees before you choose them. The trees listed in the following pages are all great options.

The benefit of growing trees indoors means that you do not need to worry about environmental factors such as storms or extreme winds blowing them over. However, growing bonsai indoors comes with its own set of unique challenges. Two of the biggest mistakes beginners make is either placing their trees near a radiator that dries them out too quickly, or putting them in dimly lit rooms. Remember that most trees require at least six hours of bright light per day. If this is not possible in your home, then it may be a good idea to supplement with some grow lights (see page 43).

Japanese holly (*Ilex crenata*)
Dark green, glossy leaves with charming, scalloped edges are a feature of this hardy evergreen. In the summer it produces delicate white flowers that mature into black berries later in the year. While it thrives best outdoors, it can adapt to indoor conditions if kept in a cool room with lots of light. During winter it is a good idea to bring it indoors and place it in a colder room between 5°C (41°F) and 10°C (50°F), allowing it to enter a natural dormancy period for optimal health and growth.

Pomegranate (*Punica granatum*)
A deciduous tree known for its narrow, oval leaves, and its striking orange-red flowers, which are followed by small pomegranate fruit. The dwarf variety *nana* is ideal for bonsai, with the best traits for miniature growth, but you can also create a creditable bonsai using a seed from a supermarket pomegranate. Indoors, place it in a well-lit spot that receives plenty of full sun during the growing season to encourage flowering. If possible, move it outdoors in the summer to give it a spell in full sunlight. In winter, when it loses its leaves and enters dormancy, keep it in a cool area such as a garage or basement to maintain temperatures between 2°C (36°F) and 4°C (39°F).

Mediterranean olive (*Olea europaea*)
This mediterranean evergreen is loved for its gnarled trunk and craggy bark, but it also has beautiful silvery-green oval-shaped leaves. It grows best outdoors but can be grown indoors with the proper care. An olive tree needs full sun to ensure its leaves stay small and it can tolerate high temperatures. In summer, it is a good idea to place an olive tree in a south-facing window so it can get sunlight all day. In winter, it is best kept at temperatures between 0°C (32°F) and 5°C (41°F) so that it can enter dormancy.

Chinese privet (*Ligustrum sinense*)
Known for its dense, glossy foliage and small oval leaves that create a full lush appearance, this is a hardy, fast-growing tree. It does well in bright, indirect light and adapts easily to various conditions. In summer place it outdoors occasionally to enjoy some direct sunlight and fresh air. In winter, keep this tree between 1°C (34°F) and 10°C (50°F); it will still need lots of light so placing it by a window in an unheated room is ideal.

Tree of a thousand stars (*Serissa japonica*)

Small white flowers that bloom in summer give this delicate evergreen its name – tree of a thousand stars. It is also loved for its flaky bark. From experience this can be a tricky tree to keep alive. It does well in a consistent spot away from drafts since sudden shifts in light, humidity or temperature can lead to leaf drop. In summer it will benefit from a spell outdoors, and once it is dormant in winter it needs to stay at a temperature between 10°C (50°F) and 20°C (68°F).

Five more bonsai for sunny spots indoors:

- Mastic tree (*Pistacia lentiscus*)
- African baobab (*Adansonia digitata*)
- Bougainvillea (*Bougainvillea glabra*)
- Chinese yew (*Podocarpus chinensis*)
- Crape myrtle (*Lagerstroemia indica*)

Overwintering bonsai

When I first got into bonsai, I saw the word 'overwintering' and thought it was a big, complicated process. Then I discovered that in reality it is pretty simple! Overwintering is the process we use to help our bonsai through the cold winter months.

Natural survivors

Some species can survive in colder temperatures, so always research the specific trees you have to find out their particular requirements.

THE RIGHT ENVIRONMENT FOR DORMANCY

Your first instinct may be to think: 'I will just bring my bonsai indoors to protect them from the cold.' While this may seem like a good idea, it can do more harm than good. There is a good chance that your trees will end their period of dormancy too early or even not start, leading to stress and weak growth. Outdoor trees must be enabled to become dormant in winter. It helps them conserve energy and prepares them for a strong growing season the following year. This involves allowing trees to become cold enough to enter dormancy – but not so cold that it damages them. If you live in a warmer climate, where temperatures do not fall below -4°C (25°F) then, in general, your trees should be fine to live outdoors. If you live in a much colder climate, with temperatures below -10°C (14°F), you should seriously consider protecting your trees in winter.

Opposite: A dormant American hornbeam (*Carpinus caroliniana*) bonsai forest overwintering outdoors in a sheltered spot. Letting trees experience seasonal cold helps trigger a healthy dormancy and supports strong growth.

PROTECTING YOUR BONSAI IN WINTER

Consider moving your trees into an unheated greenhouse, cold frame (a glazed box) or even an unheated garage or basement to protect them from the frost. Just make sure the greenhouse or cold frame does not become too hot on cold but sunny days. Trees that lose their leaves for the winter do not need any light then as they do not photosynthesize. You can also take your bonsai off your benches and move them closer to the ground to protect them from the colder winds. If you have concrete in your garden, do not allow your bonsai to sit in direct contact with the ground as the temperature can drop rapidly and freeze the trees' roots. I like to sit my trees on top of some wood. Frost blankets can also be used to prevent your bonsai from getting too cold. Wrap the trees in a breathable, insulating material like an old bedsheet or pillowcase.

WINTER TASKS

Before putting your trees away for the winter, it is a good idea to remove any fallen leaves from the pots and treat each bonsai with insecticide and fungicide. As temperatures rise in spring, any insects or fungal spores that remain dormant over winter can quickly become a problem. Apply a winter wash of lime sulphur diluted with water in a ratio of 20:1 to kill any overwintering insects, bacteria or fungi. Always follow the safety instructions on the label. Remember that although your bonsai need less water in winter, the soil should not be allowed to completely dry out.

Snow offers protection

Do not worry if your evergreen trees are covered in snow in winter, this snow acts as insulation to protect the foliage from the frost.

Opposite: A snow-covered bonsai in winter dormancy. Raise pots off the ground to protect roots from freezing, and consider moving trees indoors if temperatures drop below –10°C (14°F).

The bonsai bench

Building a stage for your trees

One of my favourite things about bonsai is going outside in the morning to look at and enjoy my trees. Having a dedicated display really enhances the bonsai experience; it allows me to appreciate my trees anew, almost as if I am at an exhibition. This is an uncomplicated build! I must emphasize that I am not a professional builder/carpenter, and this is simply how I made my bench.

1 **Preparing the space**
Clear the section of outdoor space you would like to use to ensure that you have a flat, clean and solid surface to build on. You should also pick a spot that gets direct sunlight throughout the day and near your water supply for easy watering. In the cleared area collect together the bonsai you plan to display, to get a sense of how big the bench should be (opposite, top left).

Available space

If you're working with a smaller garden or limited space, you can adjust the bench size by placing the cinderblocks closer together and cutting the decking boards with a saw to fit.

2 **Planning the bench**
Once you have measured the space you can work out how many cinderblocks you need (opposite, top right). For the example shown in these pages – which measures 3.3 × 1m (11 × 3ft) – I used 21 cinderblocks, each measuring 20 × 20 × 17cm (7 × 7 × 6in).

3 **Preparing the boards**
Next work out how many planks of wood are required. For this bench I used six planks of treated decking board, and cut them to size – each of which measured 3.3m × 15cm (11ft × 6in) after I cut them down (opposite, bottom).

4 **Place the blocks**

When placing the blocks, adjust them to ensure that they do not wobble. I have arranged the blocks so that my bench has two tiers at different heights (opposite, top left). If it is a longer bench, add blocks to the centre as I have done here for extra support. The planks should be a good distance apart but not too far apart that it will cause your bench to bow down. Have the blocks on one side slightly higher than the other so that water can run off. To do this, place a piece of wood or flat stone slab under the blocks at one side of the bench.

5 **Placing the planks**

My bench has two tiers and each one requires three planks. Sit the planks on top of the blocks, making sure they are neatly aligned with each other (opposite, top right). The weight of your trees should be enough to keep them in place. Fixing runners underneath the planks will prevent them from twisting and warping over time. To do this you will need some 3 × 2in (7.5 × 5cm) lengths of wood. Simply screw them to the underside of your planks before you sit them on top of the blocks.

6 **Protecting your bench**

Over time algae might build up on your bench. To remove it, I recommend using a decking-board cleaner/algae remover. Do this in an area away from your trees because you do not want any chemicals harming your bonsai and ensure all cleaner has been thoroughly washed off. After this, to keep your bench in good condition, apply wood stain and seal the end grain once a year. This is best done in the summer when the wood is dry. Before placing your trees on the bench, ensure that the stain has fully dried (opposite, bottom).

Arranging your trees

It is up to you how you arrange your trees. I have placed all mine quite close together for a busier look. For a more elegant effect, which allows you to enjoy each tree, space them out on the shelves.

Five outdoor bonsai for sunny gardens

The majority of bonsai should be kept outdoors since this is how trees have evolved to grow. They need real sunlight, wind and even nighttime temperature drops. They do best when exposed to all the seasons too. However, some trees thrive when exposed to direct sunlight while others prefer some shade.

Some trees are naturally adapted to thrive in direct sunlight because it's crucial for their growth and survival. In their native environments, these trees have evolved to harness the full power of the sun for photosynthesis, the process they use to convert light into energy. Sometimes you can tell just by looking what kind of growing conditions a tree likes. For example, trees that love bright areas usually have thicker or waxy leaves or needles and robust bark that is deeper and usually more resilient to strong sunlight.

Chinese elm (*Ulmus parvifolia*)

This popular species is semi-evergreen when grown indoors and is loved for its small leaves with their serrated edges. Chinese elm is perfect for beginners because it grows fast. Although it can be grown indoors if the conditions are right, I believe it is much easier to care for if kept outside. In the summer Chinese elm thrive in full sun as long as they are watered regularly. Although it can tolerate some frost, in winter keep the bonsai in an environment where temperatures stay between 1°C (34°F) and 10°C (50°F).

Buttonwood (*Conocarpus erectus*)

This tropical evergreen does best in full sun and can grow pretty quickly. It is known for its dramatic trunk movement and textured bark. Buttonwoods have thick leathery leaves with a soft silvery underside that adds a unique colour contrast. They lend themselves well to many bonsai styles, but my favourite is the informal upright. It grows best in well-draining soil and does not tolerate cold temperatures. In winter, this species must be kept indoors or in a heated greenhouse when temperatures drop below 10°C (50°F).

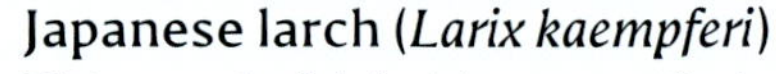

Japanese larch (*Larix kaempferi*)

This wonderful deciduous conifer is probably one of my favourite outdoor trees. It has fine, delicate green leaves that look like pine needles which turn a golden yellow/orange before the tree loses them for the winter. I recommend this bonsai to beginners because it is hard to kill, grows fast and has nice flexible branches. It does best in full sun during the growing season but requires lots of water. It is frost tolerant and I have found that, in winter, it does best in temperatures between -10°C (14°F) and 5°C (41°F) to ensure it becomes dormant.

Chinese juniper '*Itoigawa*' (*Juniperus chinensis* 'itoigawa')

This gem of a juniper cultivar is a sought-after bonsai because it has a dense growth pattern with a vibrant green scaly foliage, stunning deadwood and vibrant red-coloured bark. As an evergreen, it keeps its foliage all year round. Although these bonsai can be expensive, they are relatively easy to care for and style since the branches tend to be flexible for a longer time than other trees. In the summer, junipers benefit from full sun, and this helps keep their foliage nice and compact. In winter, I try to keep my junipers at a temperature between -10°C (14°F) and 4°C (39°F).

Fuji cherry (*Prunus incisa* '*Kojo-no-mai*')
This delicate deciduous species is adored for its beautiful pink and white blossoms that emerge in spring and cover all its branches. Once the flowers fall off, it grows small, oval, finely toothed leaves that turn a golden orange and then red in autumn. It thrives in full sun as long as it is watered regularly, especially on particularly hot days. This exposure to lots of sun helps maximize flower production. Once a Fuji cherry has lost its leaves in winter, I like to keep it between -5°C (23°F) and 5°C (41°F) to ensure it becomes dormant, although these trees are quite frost-hardy.

Five more trees for sunny gardens:

- Cotoneaster (*Cotoneaster horizontalis*)
- Japanese quince (*Chaenomeles japonica*)
- Nagasaki crab apple (*Malus cerasifera*)
- Japanese white pine (*Pinus parviflora*)
- Japanese cedar (*Cryptomeria japonica*)

Rooting for Success

Healthy roots are crucial if you want a tree to flourish, and the secret to this is the right balance of water and oxygen. Soil is also important if your tree is to thrive, and so you'll learn how to make your own soil mix. Knowing the best way to fertilize a bonsai is vital too.

Root-pruning checklist

Deciding which roots to remove can be a little confusing if you aren't sure what the goal is. The aim is simply to promote lateral growing roots that will develop into nice *nebari* each time you work on them. The following guide should help to make root pruning easier and give you an understanding of how to create good root structure.

Even root distribution

Remember to balance the root flare. If a tree has more growth on one side than the other, prune back more heavily on the stronger side so that when it grows again, the energy is distributed evenly. This will give you more root density, which helps when it is time to put it into a small bonsai pot.

It's ideal to gently wash a tree's roots before pruning, so you can see their structure more clearly. However, not all trees respond well to having their roots washed. Root work can vary depending on the species, especially for those where bare-rooting isn't done and the roots are harder to see. In these cases, extra care is needed to manage the roots properly. Feel with your fingers for where the roots are emerging and the direction in which they flow. If your tree has been sitting in overly wet soil and some roots are rotting, remove these first. Then rake out the remaining roots working laterally from the base of the trunk, and study them, to see which need to be pruned. There are two main types of roots: feeder roots and stability roots. The most important are the feeder roots. These are the finer roots that absorb water and nutrients. Then there are the thicker roots, whose main job is to provide stability; these are not as vital and can be pruned off (unless you are keeping those on the surface *nebari*).

What to prune

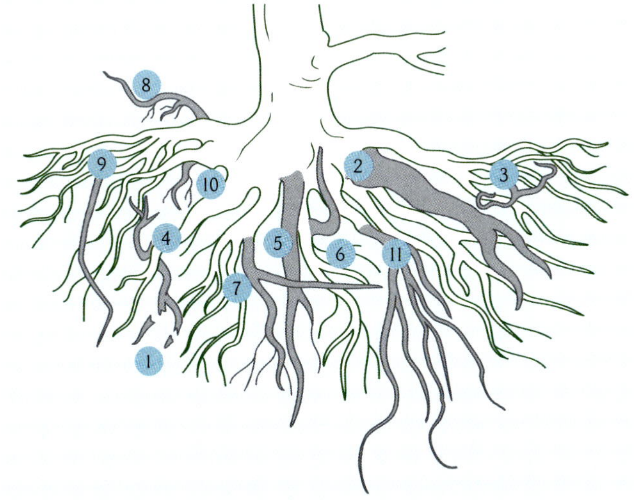

1. Rotting or dead roots.
2. Overly thick stabilizing (or tap) roots under the *nebari*.
3. Crossing/curling roots.
4. Roots growing straight up.
5. Roots growing straight down.
6. Roots growing towards the trunk.
7. Roots that split awkwardly and ruin the radial pattern.
8. Roots emerging from above the *nebari* line.
9. Roots growing at strange, steep angles without purpose.
10. Growth that is too high to reveal more of the lower trunk and to expose the *nebari*.
11. Extra-long feeder roots.

Watering wisdom: how to keep your bonsai hydrated

Watering is one of the most important things that you can do for a bonsai. It is not especially complicated, but it is crucial that it is done correctly to ensure your tree remains healthy and happy. For beginners, one of the main reasons a tree dies is improper watering.

Opposite: Harvested rainwater is an excellent source of water; bonsai artist Attila Csintalan uses a barrel with a pump to collect his rainwater. It must be cleaned occasionally to avoid fungal build-up. This Scots pine (*Pinus sylvestris*) is being hydrated with rainwater.

KEEP IT SIMPLE

A lot of people overcomplicate watering, and there are even guides that say a particular tree must be watered a certain number of times a week, when this is not the case at all. The amount of water a tree needs depends on many factors, and each one is different. How much water the soil holds, the species of tree, the humidity, and the temperature all contribute to how much water is lost from a bonsai.

To determine the quantity of water a tree needs, a rule of thumb I like to follow is this: the soil should be moist, not overly wet, and never allowed to dry out completely. A good way to test this is to feel the soil with your finger. If it is soggy, leave it to dry some more before the next watering. If it is bone dry, water it immediately and hope it survives. If it feels moist, this is the sweet spot. Remember, roots that dry out will die, while those that stay in very wet conditions can suffocate and rot. Also take care that the drip trays that come with a bonsai do not cause the roots to rot. After watering, empty the tray so that the bottom of the pot does not sit in a puddle of water.

Five bonsai that love a drink

Some trees thrive in very wet environments and require more watering to stay healthy. These are known as high-water mobility trees and they absorb and transport water very efficiently. If you live in a rainy climate like I do, these trees may be for you.

High-water mobility trees evolved in environments where lots of water is available. They tend to dry out faster and therefore need to be watered more often or will require the soil to hold more moisture. If you prefer trees that need regular watering, these water-loving species are an excellent choice for your bonsai collection. Remember, all trees are unique and have slightly different requirements so research your specific species before jumping right in.

A common mistake that beginners make is to water a tree too much. The advantage of high-water mobility trees is that they are resilient to overwatering. This makes them great for first-time bonsai owners who can sometimes be too hands-on with bonsai care and are still learning about balance. Using a soil type that retains water for longer is helpful for growing these species. A soil that doesn't retain moisture for long can still work well if the tree is watered more frequently.

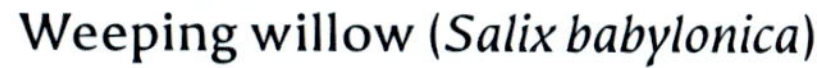

Weeping willow (*Salix babylonica*)

This deciduous species is loved for its graceful weeping branches and oval-shaped leaves. It is a great one for beginners because it grows so fast and you can get such quick results. It is naturally found near rivers and lakes and requires constant moisture to thrive. Weeping willow does well in a deep pot with high moisture-retaining soil such as a mixture of compost and perlite. Regular pruning is important to keep this bonsai's growth under control and, in the summer, it may even need multiple waterings every day.

Korean hornbeam (*Carpinus turczaninovii*)

A highly sought-after deciduous species loved for its small, folded, oval-shaped leaves that produce vibrant autumn colours. It responds well to pruning during the growing season and does particularly well in soil that is consistently moist. It benefits from frequent pruning, resulting in good ramification (see page 99) and dense foliage. Consistent watering is essential for this species since it does not like its soil to be too dry for too long. In winter it requires protection from extreme cold.

Swamp white oak (*Quercus bicolor*)

As the name suggests, this deciduous species is naturally found growing in wetlands and floodplains. It has broad, oval-shaped leaves with shallow, rounded lobes. These trees are more proportionally suited to be larger-sized bonsai since the leaves are naturally large. They do well in a free-draining soil that includes a mix of pumice, akadama and lava rock (see page 72), which provides good aeration while still retaining moisture. It requires frequent watering, especially during the growing season, sometimes two to three times a day in summer.

Japanese zelkova (*Zelkova serrata*)

The fine, serrated leaves of this deciduous species turn a beautiful vibrant red in autumn. I have often seen them developed as a broom-style bonsai as their delicate branches can easily be trained to have good ramification. It generally tolerates most soil types, though it does best in soil that is more water-retentive. Regular watering is crucial, particularly in the warmer summer months, since dry soil can quickly lead to leaf scorch and weaker growth.

Five more bonsai that love a drink:

- Black birch (*Betula nigra*)
- Norway spruce (*Picea abies*)
- Red maple (*Acer rubrum*)
- Buttonwood (*Conocarpus erectus*)
- Bald or swamp cypress (*Taxodium distichum*)

Dawn redwood (*Metasequoia glyptostroboides*)

Fossil records for this deciduous conifer date back more than 50 million years. It has delicate, feathery foliage that turns vibrant orange before being shed for the winter. The tree thrives in wet conditions and grows super-fast. This makes it an excellent species as a beginner's bonsai but make sure you have time to keep on top of watering because its roots can dry out quickly, especially during the growing season. I like to add a little sphagnum moss into the soil mix to keep the humidity levels up.

Bonsai soil secrets: what is under the surface?

Below: If your tree comes in pure compost, repot it into a soil that is more free-draining as pure compost tends to compact quickly and can stay too wet for too long which leads to root rot.

Every bonsai artist has their own special soil mix that works for them. While you can follow their advice I also recommend experimenting to see what works best in your specific growing conditions.

THE GOAL WITH BONSAI SOIL

A good bonsai soil mix should offer a balanced distribution of water and oxygen. This is achieved through a granular mix with even particle sizes that retain moisture yet drain well and maintain structural integrity. A quality soil mix will include components with a high cation exchange capacity (CEC), allowing the soil to retain nutrients from fertilizers and release them gradually to the roots.

Opposite: A high-quality bonsai soil such as akadama offers excellent drainage while also retaining moisture and nutrients. It gradually releases nutrients to the roots, supporting healthy growth over time.

MY TRIED-AND-TESTED SOIL COMPONENTS

Akadama

One of the most popular bonsai components, akadama is a naturally occurring clay-like mineral that is mined from volcanic regions in Japan and comes in various grades. I use the deeper mined akadama that has been exposed to hotter temperatures and is naturally semi-fired. It achieves a soil that breaks down slowly compared to akadama mined from shallower areas which is softer and degrades in as little as one year.

Kanuma

Another material mined in the volcanic regions in Japan, kanuma is used for acid-loving trees including azaleas. It has a pH of around 5.5 and can be incorporated into a soil mix to make it slightly more acidic. Many people plant azaleas directly into a mix of kanuma and sphagnum moss. It holds moisture well.

Perlite

This is a type of volcanic glass that expands into light and aerated granules when heated. It is a good addition to a soil mix, particularly if you want to improve drainage and aeration.

A pumice alternative

Some people use cat litter as a cheap alternative to pumice. If you do this, use the molar-clay form since anything else will become mushy. Also make sure it's the plain, unscented and non-clumping type without added chemicals or perfumes that could harm your tree.

Pumice

This is a type of volcanic rock that helps to improve soil drainage and aeration. It can hold water well and keep the roots of your bonsai moist while also providing great soil structure. The rough texture of the particles allows roots to grip onto it easily.

Composted pine bark (organic matter)

This component is beneficial for trees with high water mobility, or for bonsai grown in a hotter climate. Using organic matter can help to increase water retention. I prefer composted pine bark because the particles are larger than in regular compost, which can clog pot drainage.

Lava rock

Found in volcanic regions, in bonsai soil this is mainly used for faster drainage. It has a porous nature that allows for a lot of aeration and root anchoring.

Mixing magic:
DIY bonsai soil recipes

Pumice

Your soil mix may differ from mine thanks to your climate and growing conditions. If you live in a particularly arid region, you may choose to add more organic matter to help retain moisture. Since rainfall is high where I live in Northern Ireland, I prefer an inorganic, free-draining mix to prevent waterlogging and root rot.

Akadama

Lava rock

1 Choose your soil components

I use pumice, semi-fired akadama and lava rock for my standard bonsai soil mix (below left). Each component plays a crucial role in maintaining a healthy root system. Pumice retains moisture while allowing excess water to drain, and its rough surface allows the roots to attach to it easily. Semi-fired akadama provides excellent water retention and nutrient absorption, gradually releasing fertilizers to the tree's roots. Unlike regular akadama, the semi-fired version breaks down more slowly which maintains soil structure for longer. Lava rock enhances drainage and increases oxygen in the roots. This mix ensures a good balance of water and oxygen.

2 Mix your soil ratio

When mixing my bonsai soil (below centre), I usually use a 1:1:1 ratio (equal parts of each ingredient). You can adjust this mix based on the tree species, or even experiment with different ratios to see how your trees respond in your environment. If you are developing a pre-bonsai (a plant about to be trained into a bonsai) and using a basic mix of compost and perlite, you may want to increase the amount of compost for trees that need more moisture. This helps retain water longer, meaning you will not have to water as often. For trees that prefer free-draining soil, reducing the compost and increasing the perlite component will improve drainage and prevent overwatering issues.

3 Organic mixes for arid climates

If you live in a very warm and dry climate and need soil that holds a lot of water, you can create a more organic mix by using a blend of pine bark and perlite. Simply sift the perlite to remove all of the fine particles and mix it in a 1:1 ratio with pine bark. This blend can also be used for trees that have high water mobility if you do not want to have to water these trees two to three times a day in the hotter months.

Size matters

If you use granular soil, make sure all the particles are around the same size. This ensures good and consistent drainage and prevents compaction. Before repotting a tree, I recommend sieving out fine particles and dust from your substrate (below right) because these can settle at the bottom of the pot, restrict airflow and cause drainage issues.

Fertilizer 101: what, when and how to feed your tree

Fertilization is just as important to your tree as water. Without the correct nutrients in the soil, its health could suffer. Just like everything in bonsai, the correct balance is key to a happy plant.

ESSENTIAL NUTRIENTS – NPK

When you fertilize a tree, you are not feeding it in the way you might feed yourself. Trees make their own food through photosynthesis, a process that uses sunlight to change carbon dioxide and water into oxygen and glucose, a type of sugar that fuels their growth. Fertilizers provide essential nutrients that the tree needs to stay healthy and grow properly. They help improve soil quality and the tree's ability to produce its own food. There are many different types of fertilizer on the market, and it can be very confusing to work out which one you need for your bonsai. Every fertilizer has an NPK value. This is the ratio of the three essential elements of any fertilizer – nitrogen (N), phosphorus (P) and potassium (K). These play a vital role in the development of your trees.

Opposite: Fertilizer baskets like this one feeding a Chinese juniper 'Itoigawa' (*Juniperus chinensis* 'Itoigawa') allow you to put solid fertilizer inside to protect it from animals or from rolling off the pot as you water.

Nitrogen for strength

Nitrogen is responsible for strong growth in the leaves and stems. A bonsai with a good level of nitrogen in the soil will grow more vigorously with strong green foliage. If your tree does not get enough nitrogen, the leaves may grow too weak to survive. Too much nitrogen is toxic and can burn the delicate roots.

Phosphorus for roots and flowers

To build strength not only in the internal structure of your bonsai but also more growth at the apex, you need phosphorus. It also aids root growth and can encourage better flowering in trees such as azaleas.

Potassium for health and resilience

The overall health of your bonsai relies on potassium. It aids water regulation, nutrient transport and strong root development. The right potassium levels are crucial not only for flowering but for fruit development and maturation, vital if you want to grow attractive fruit on your trees.

Micronutrients

It is a good idea to buy a fertilizer that shows the amounts of micronutrients it contains. This will list trace amounts of elements such as iron, magnesium, calcium and zinc that do amazing things for your trees, including supporting chlorophyll production, enzyme function and disease resistance.

TYPES OF FERTILIZER

Liquid fertilizer acts fast and is easily absorbed by the roots; however it must be used more often than other fertilizers.

Solid fertilizers are put on the surface of the soil and slowly release nutrients over time with every watering.

Organic fertilizers come from natural sources including bonemeal, seaweed, manure and fish emulsion. These enrich the soil while also feeding your tree.

Chemical fertilizers are synthetic and give you more precise control of the nutrients. They do not improve soil health and if overused can lead to salt buildup in the soil.

FEEDING YOUR BONSAI

The type of fertilizer you use for your bonsai not only depends on the time of year (see page 86) but also on its stage of development. For example: a tree in training benefits from a higher nitrogen fertilizer (10:6:6 NPK) to encourage strong growth, more side shoots and back budding. A tree in refinement, however, requires slower growth with shorter spaces between the nodes on the stems, and a more balanced fertilizer (6:6:6 NPK) is ideal.

Balanced fertilization preferred

Chinese juniper 'Itoigawa' bonsai (*Juniperus chinensis* 'Itoigawa') thrive with balanced fertilization. While they don't require as much nitrogen as fast-growing species, a moderate, well-rounded NPK ratio supports healthy foliage and encourages the development of strong, woody branches.

Above: A healthy ficus (*Ficus microcarpa* 'Ginseng') with dark green, glossy leaves. This popular indoor species is actually a grafted bonsai made by combining two different *Ficus* species. They are known for their thick, bulbous roots at the base. Good bonsai care is key to keeping them strong.

Common mistakes: signs you are over- or underfeeding

Fertilization is not that complicated once you understand what each of the nutrients is responsible for, but overfeeding and underfeeding can cause problems. Recognizing a nutrient imbalance will help you tweak your fertilizing routine to keep your bonsai happy.

If a tree is unwell due to pests or fungus (see pages 180–4), 99 per cent of the time it is best not to fertilize it. Fertilizer is not a cure for a sick tree and can often do more harm than good. In these cases, it is best to simply water the tree as needed and let it recover naturally.

SIGNS OF OVERFEEDING

Too much fertilizer can burn roots and cause mineral buildup in the soil; this is due to the use of too much nitrogen, especially in early spring. As a result, your tree may produce weak, leggy growth. Leaf burn and yellowing foliage are signs of root damage. If using chemical fertilizers, you might also notice mineral deposits forming on the soil surface. Leaf burn or salt damage is almost always caused by synthetic fertilizers at a ratio higher than the recommended amount. It is nearly impossible to use too much organic fertilizer.

Solution: Flush the soil with clean water to remove excess minerals and fertilize less frequently.

SIGNS OF UNDERFEEDING

A lack of nutrients can weaken a tree, slow its growth and make it more prone to pests and diseases. Signs to look for include chlorosis (light yellowing leaves due to nitrogen deficiency), stunted growth and, in severe cases, leaf drop and branch dieback.

Solution: Ensure your bonsai is fertilized regularly.

Above left: Signs of overfeeding in bonsai, which can include yellowing leaves and leaf burn. This is often caused by excessive nitrogen or mineral buildup from synthetic fertilizers.

Above right: Chlorosis and leaf drop in a bonsai are typical symptoms of underfeeding. A lack of nutrients, especially nitrogen, can weaken the tree and reduce growth.

Timing is everything: when and when not to fertilize

Below: The seasonal growth cycle of a deciduous bonsai. Fertilizer should be applied during the active growth phases of spring and summer, and reduced or stopped in autumn and winter when the tree is dormant.

Fertilizing at the correct time is important to keep your bonsai healthy and happy. Knowing when to fertilize ensures your bonsai gets exactly what it needs, when it needs it. If you feed too early or too late in the year, it can stress the tree or not give you the results you want.

THE SCIENCE OF FERTILIZING

Timing is everything with bonsai and this is particularly important for fertilization. Trees follow a natural growth cycle that is influenced by the seasons and their hormones. Many trees experience two main phases in their cycle: dormancy and

growth. During dormancy, their nutrient uptake slows down as they prepare for the winter. This is controlled by the hormone abscisic acid (ABA), which signals to the tree to stop growing and conserve its energy. Fertilizing a tree in the winter is ineffective, and fertilizing in autumn with too much nitrogen can delay dormancy. This can lead to weak growth and a stressed tree that will not survive in freezing conditions.

In spring, as the temperature warms up, ABA levels drop. The hormones cytokinins (responsible for cell division) and auxins (responsible for elongation of branches and root growth) take over and the tree enters a period of active growth. This is the best time to start fertilizing to fuel growth and encourage good branch development. As the year moves into summer, growth slows a little and trees focus on thickening their trunks and strengthening their roots. Continue to fertilize; I sometimes switch to a more balanced fertilizer (10:10:10 NPK) depending on how the tree is developing.

Fertilizing a tree immediately after repotting with a lower-nitrogen organic fertilizer can be beneficial, but avoid using high-nitrogen synthetic fertilizers right after repotting.

When not to fertilize

These are the general rules I follow:

- Do not fertilize a stressed tree unless the stress was caused by a lack of nutrients.
- Do not fertilize dormant trees.
- In most cases, do not fertilize immediately after repotting.
- Do not fertilize in extreme heat or drought.
- Do not fertilize compacted soil.

Autumn

Winter

Period of dormancy

Fertilizing routines and regimens

Below: The Arakawa Japanese maple (*Acer palmatum* 'Arakawa') is a unique Japanese maple that is instantly recognizable and loved for its aged-looking, craggy bark that develops as it matures.

Fertilizing is not complicated if you have a good regimen and implement it consistently. Trees require a different routine depending on if they are tropical, deciduous, evergreen or a species that prefers a more acidic soil, however, once you know the specific needs of your tree, fertilization is pretty straightforward.

Tropical and sub-tropical bonsai

Species from warmer countries do not really enter dormancy. Sometimes they may experience a period of reduced growth, but tropical trees need consistent fertilization all year round. During their most active growth periods, in spring and summer, I use a balanced dilute liquid fertilizer (10:10:10 NPK) with every watering. In the colder months, I reduce how often I feed tropical bonsai to every three days but do not stop completely. Even though they are sometimes classed differently by sellers, sub-tropical bonsai should be fertilized in the same way as tropical ones as they do not go fully dormant in the way that deciduous and evergreen trees do.

Diluted liquid fertilizer

Deciduous and evergreen bonsai

These trees go through periods of active and dormant growth and must be fed accordingly. Generally, start fertilizing in spring with a high-nitrogen fertilizer. As it comes into summer, I like to switch to a balanced fertilizer and then, as autumn arrives, I feed with a low-nitrogen fertilizer that helps to prepare the trees for dormancy.

High nitrogen fertilizer

Lime-intolerant bonsai

Use this fertilizing regimen for species including azalea, camellia and blueberries. Lime-free fertilizers that are high in phosphorus and potassium work best for these trees. They are easy to find if you look for a fertilizer that is designed for ericaceous plants (ones that struggle to grow in alkaline or lime-rich conditions) in a garden centre or bonsai nursery.

Lime-free slow release fertilizer

Yearly fertilizing regimen

This chart provides a general guide as to when and what to feed your bonsai with throughout the year. In spring and summer use a high-nitrogen fertilizer to support strong leaf and branch growth. As autumn arrives, switch to a low-nitrogen fertilizer to encourage root strength and prepare the tree for dormancy. During winter, most trees should not be fertilized at all especially if they are deciduous and not actively growing.

However, tropical species can still be fertilized lightly year-round with a balanced fertilizer because they do not go fully dormant. Adjust your feeding based on how your tree is growing and always follow the product instructions.

Tree Type	Spring	Summer	Autumn	Winter
Evergreens 	H	H	L	
Tropical 	B	B	B	B
Deciduous 	H	H	L	
Lime intolerant 	H	H	L	

B Balanced fertilizer H High-nitrogen fertilizer L Low-nitrogen fertilizer

MY FERTILIZING REGIMEN

I fertilize tropical species such as *Ficus* all year round, using a balanced liquid chemical fertilizer with every watering. I keep these trees indoors and do not use any organic products that might make my house smell bad! In winter I ease off the fertilizer and only use it once a week until spring returns. For deciduous and evergreen trees, such as maples and junipers, I place organic solid fertilizer pellets on top of the soil during the growing season, which will break down and feed the tree every time I water; others slowly release nutrients every time the tree is watered. On top of this, I alternate fertilizing once every second week with a seaweed and fish emulsion – one week seaweed and the next fish emulsion. I feed lime-intolerant trees such as Satsuki azalea *(Rhododendron indicum)* with a chemical ericaceous fertilizer (designed for acidic soils) once a week during the growing season. I also fertilize them with seaweed once a week, and occasionally mist the foliage with an Epsom salts solution (see page 89).

Above left: Fertilizer pellets slowly release nutrients into the soil as water passes over them, providing a steady supply to the roots of a Fuji cherry (*Prunus incisa* 'Kojo-no-mai').

Above right: Liquid fertilizers such as fish emulsion and seaweed extract can be watered in to quickly feed your tree – here a Japanese holly (*Ilex crenata*) – during the growing season.

Time for an uplift

Foliar feeding is useful if a tree needs a little boost or is recovering after a repot when the newly pruned roots mean that it is unsafe to fertilize the soil.

Foliar feeding and the Epsom salts trick

Foliar feeding – misting nutrients onto the leaves of a plant – has its uses in bonsai, but it is not a solution for a tree that is suffering from a nutrient deficiency. It is a method that complements, but should not replace, regular root fertilization.

THE ROLE OF FOLIAR FEEDING

When a dilute solution of a liquid fertilizer is gently sprayed onto the leaves of a bonsai, it is quickly absorbed through the stomata (pores) in the leaves and this can help you to diagnose whether a tree has a soil-nutrient deficiency. If once the fertilizer has been applied any signs of dicolouraton go away, then you know the bonsai was low in nutrients.

THE EPSOM SALTS TRICK

By using Epsom salts (yes, magnesium sulphate, the same kind we use in the bath for muscle soreness), you can instantly enhance your bonsai's foliage. You can try this before an exhibition, perhaps, or if your trees need a quick boost to green up their leaves.

Dissolve 7g (¼oz) of Epsom salts in 1 litre (1¾ pints) of water and use this solution to mist the foliage. Within 30 minutes the leaves will appear greener and more vibrant thanks to the mineral being a key component in chlorophyll production. This mixture is especially beneficial for azaleas, which need a little more magnesium than some other plant species. Regular use of this mixture can dramatically improve their blooms and keep their foliage happy.

Leaves only

I do not recommend using the Epsom salts solution in soil since it can compete with calcium uptake. It is purely a supplement and should never replace a proper fertilization routine.

Opposite: A mature, healthy Korean hornbeam (*Carpinus turczaninovii*) in full leaf with a well-developed trunk and exposed surface roots.

Shaping your bonsai's story

Successful bonsai are usually inspired by the natural world. When you're ready to style a tree, start by visualizing what you want to accomplish and spend time outdoors looking for inspiration. Then use basic pruning and wiring techniques to express your tree's beauty.

Shaping techniques: clip-and-grow vs wiring

There are two main ways to shape a bonsai: clip-and-grow or wiring the branches into the desired position. Most people use a combination of these techniques to achieve the tree they want.

CLIP-AND-GROW

Pruning using clip-and-grow is as easy as it sounds – just prune a branch or trunk and then let it grow. Pruning refers to any cutting used to shape, maintain or reduce the size of a tree and can include branch removal, defoliation or fine wiring adjustments. With clip-and-grow, the tree is shaped by repeatedly allowing shoots to grow before cutting them back to a desired point. This encourages better taper, branch placement and natural structure without heavy wiring. It takes longer than wiring, but many people prefer it for its more organic look.

WIRING

To shape a tree with wire, simply wrap aluminium or copper wire around a tree's branches or trunk, then bend it into the desired position (see page 112). Aluminium wire is a lot cheaper and easier to use and a good choice if you are a beginner and need some practice. Copper wire is used on conifers and pines. It is a little trickier to handle than aluminium because the wire hardens as you use it, and it becomes less malleable once it has been wired and difficult to unwire if you make a mistake.

Opposite

Top left: Identifying where to prune an Eastern white cedar (*Thuja occidentalis*).

Top right: Clip-and-grow encourages dense branching and natural shaping without wire on this Eastern white cedar.

Bottom left: Aluminium wire applied to a Japanese larch (*Larix kaempferi*), helping shape young branches into position.

Bottom right: Trees such as this Japanese larch are best wired right before the buds open in early spring; this way, you do not damage the delicate foliage as it starts to grow.

Prevent scars

To avoid scarring the bark once a branch has set, simply cut the wire off piece by piece rather than unwinding it.

The art of pruning: sculpting your tree

No bonsai is ever truly finished. Trees are living things that continue to grow and so, even when you have achieved the desired form, a tree will continue to grow and develop. There are two main types of pruning used to keep bonsai in shape: structural and maintenance.

WHEN TO PRUNE YOUR BONSAI

To ensure that a tree will recover from being pruned, it is important that it is in good health and worked on at the right time of year. Tropical species can be pruned all year round because they do not become dormant. For deciduous and evergreen trees, summer is generally the best time for maintenance pruning, and winter is an ideal time for structural pruning. By waiting until the leaves have hardened off, you allow the tree to complete its first flush of growth and stabilize its hormone levels. This way, when you prune, the disruption to auxin flow (see page 83) triggers controlled back-budding rather than stunting or confusing the tree's growth response.

Opposite: Bonsai tweezers are used here for pinching out new growth. This technique helps maintain the shape of this Chinese juniper 'Blaauw' (*Juniperus chinensis* 'Blaauw') and encourages finer branching.

STRUCTURAL PRUNING

Cutting major branches or even performing a trunk chop that changes the look and shape of a bonsai is referred to as structural pruning. This may be done to remove branches that may become an issue in the future or resolve 'problems' with a tree. When I say problems, I mean branches that do not conform to the desired design or fall within the general pruning guidelines to improve a tree (see pages 106–7). It can be done during the growing season, but to minimize stress it is best performed during winter when trees are dormant. At this time, the sap is not flowing and therefore there will not be too much bleeding from the tree. After a big cut, it is good practice to apply cut putty to prevent infection and to encourage callus formation – where the tree seals a cut by forming callus tissue around the edges of the wound.

One of the best times to remove large branches is after the first flush of growth has hardened off in late spring to early summer, as this is when callus formation is most rapid and healing is at its peak. Avoid carrying out heavy pruning in the winter when trees are dormant and cannot begin to form callus tissue, as this increases the risk of dieback around the cut site. If large branches must be removed at this time, leave a stub and make the final cut once the tree is in active growth.

MAINTENANCE PRUNING

Once your tree has a good structure, use maintenance pruning to keep it in shape. This simply involves pruning back any excess growth that goes beyond the desired silhouette. Depending on the species and health of the tree this can be done multiple times a year. Deciduous and tropical trees generally require more frequent pruning than evergreens, which are usually pruned once or twice a year. Maintenance pruning also helps to distribute the energy evenly across a tree and redirects growth inwards; this stops a tree becoming too leggy. It is also important to let your trees grow unchecked from time to time to enable them to become strong. Periodic growth spurts help the branches thicken and strengthen the tree, and letting it grow out for a while before pruning it back is crucial, especially for developing tapered branches. Obsessively pruning a tree so that it always looks good can weaken it. A well-looked-after tree goes through phases of appearing attractive for a little while and then growing wild to become strong.

TAPER AND INVERSE TAPER

Taper refers to the gradual thickening of a trunk or branch from the top to the base. A tree with good taper appears natural, stable and aged. Inverse taper is where the trunk gets thicker or swells in certain areas. It can be caused by too many branches growing in one spot and is considered undesirable since it can look juvenile and disrupt the natural visual flow. To prevent it, ensure that not too many branches grow from one spot in young trees.

Below: Bonsai shears are used to carry out maintenance pruning to refine the tree's silhouette. This regular trimming keeps the growth compact and encourages balanced development in this Chinese elm (*Ulmus parvifolia*).

Pruning deciduous bonsai

Opposite: A Japanese maple 'Katsura' (*Acer palmatum* 'Katsura') being lightly pruned in spring. Removing the terminal leaves helps to control length, encourages back-budding, and promotes finer ramification.

To maintain a compact shape on a deciduous bonsai, it is essential to manage new growth before it gets too thick since this can make your tree look unbalanced. You can do this with careful maintenance, pruning and pinching.

With deciduous bonsai, once all the major structural pruning has been completed to establish the framework for ramification, focus shifts to controlling and maintaining new growth while also ensuring the tree remains healthy and strong.

PINCHING OUT TERMINAL BUDS

If the new branches and buds that have opened in the spring are left unchecked they will keep getting longer until they become leggy. Pinching out simply involves pinching off a terminal bud or new growth. This stops the branch from extending any further and encourages back-budding, where dormant buds open and grow into new side branches, leading to a denser foliage pad and much finer ramification.

DIEBACK

Research the species of tree you are pruning since some, such as Japanese maple (*Acer palmatum*), are prone to dieback and need to be pruned accordingly. Leave a 1–2cm (½–¾in) stub above the next node rather than cutting flush with it since deciduous trees often die back to the next healthy node or bud. Remove the stub once it is dry and the wound has sealed. This prevents dieback from travelling further into the branch.

What is ramification?

This is the intricate network of fine branches that develops as a tree's limbs divide repeatedly into smaller and smaller offshoots. Ramification is about bifurcation, which occurs when a branch is pruned and then splits into two. Over time, with periods of growth and regular pruning, the new branches divide again, gradually creating a more natural-looking and refined structure.

Pruning juniper bonsai

Junipers are one of my favourite trees to work on, but as an evergreen they do require a different approach to deciduous species. At first, juniper may seem intimidating, but once you understand their growth habits and how they respond to pruning, you will be able to quickly create a nice, healthy, compact bonsai.

Below: Pinching out the soft tips of Chinese juniper (*Juniperus chinensis* 'Itoigawa') growth by hand encourages back-budding and helps maintain dense, compact foliage pads.

KEEPING IN SHAPE

Once you have completed the major structural pruning and development, use maintenance pruning to create dense foliage pads (a dense, natural-looking cluster of leaves and twigs on a branch). Pruning juniper foliage is best done when it is actively growing, but take a more cautious approach than with

deciduous trees. You can't just hack at the foliage as if you are pruning a hedge. If you do, you will cut off all of the growing tips, which greatly weakens the tree and causes it to go brown at the ends. Instead, pinch out or cut the long shoots at the base, right at the stem of the shoot. Juniper pruning is usually best done between one and three times during the growing season depending on the growth of the tree – typically in late spring/early summer and again in late summer.

THINNING

If a foliage pad becomes too dense, it must be thinned out so that light and air can reach the inner branches to encourage more back-budding to keep the tree compact. To thin out the foliage, prune back and remove any branches that are too long or are causing congestion. Once pruned you can further enhance a pad by using wire to evenly space the finer branches into a fan shape (see page 112). Remember to always leave foliage on the branch so that it will continue to live. If you prune a juniper back too aggressively and leave bare branches there is a good chance this branch will not back-bud.

Below centre: Pruning the inner growth.

Below: After pruning, the inner growth is exposed to light and air, promoting healthy back-budding and overall pad structure.

Pruning pine bonsai

Pines are unique among bonsai trees, and their pruning techniques are totally different from those used for deciduous trees and junipers. Once you understand a few simple pruning techniques for pines, you'll be well on your way to developing a compact, balanced bonsai.

The best time to prune a pine depends on whether it is a single-flush or double-flush species. Single-flush trees such as the Scots pine (*Pinus sylvestris*), should be structurally pruned in late summer, while candle (or tree shoot) pruning is best done in early summer. A good signal that it is time to do this is when small needles start to emerge from the sides of the candle. When pruning, cut the candle about halfway down, but never remove all the emerging needles or the branch tip may die off. Remember why you are candle pruning; the technique controls energy distribution to keep your tree compact. If your tree is still developing thickness let it grow freely instead.

Double-flush pines, including Japanese black pine (*Pinus thunbergii*), can be pruned once a year in early summer. Secondary candle selection can be done in early autumn as the second flush hardens off. The second flush often sees shorter and finer growth which leads to a more compact bonsai. A pine's growth habit is apically dominant, meaning they direct most energy to the top of the tree. To help balance growth, prune the upper branches more heavily and leave more shoots on the weaker lower branches (this is a good general rule to follow but do also check each candle individually and prune according to its strength/weakness).

Opposite: Candle pruning a Japanese black pine (*Pinus thunbergii*) in early summer. Cutting the candle controls energy distribution, promotes back-budding, and helps create a more compact structure.

Candle pruning

This technique involves shortening a pine tree's soft, new shoots, called candles, to control growth. This encourages back-budding and more compact growth.

Pruning azalea bonsai

There are more than 10,000 registered varieties of azalea, each with unique bloom colours, leaf shapes and growth habits.

Everyone's favourite

Satsuki azalea (*Rhododendron indicum*) is the most popular azalea for bonsai. It is prized for its small leaves, vibrant flowers and ability to bud back on old wood, making it perfect for refinement.

PRUNING

For structural pruning, azaleas can be cut back to bare wood and back-bud with no issues as long as the tree is in good health. If pruned at the wrong time, you may not get flowers in the following growing season. The flower buds form at the tips of the previous year's shoots, so if you prune at the wrong time you will cut off the next season's flowers. To avoid this, prune immediately after flowering (opposite, top left). So doing removes the wilted flowers (opposite, top right) and encourages back-budding so your tree will stay nice and compact.

DEADHEADING AZALEA

In nature, once a flower is pollinated and wilts the tree naturally directs its energy into producing fruit. This process takes up a lot of resources which the tree could otherwise use for new growth and back-budding. Deadheading azalea bonsai prevents fruit formation and allows the tree to redirect its energy into producing stronger branches, finer ramification (see page 99) and more flower buds for the next season.

THINNING FOR BALANCE

Azaleas back-bud easily which can lead to more compact growth. To maintain a well-structured tree (opposite, bottom), it is important to be selective about which branches to keep. After flowering, carefully thin out excess shoots, allowing light and air to reach the inner branches.

Bonsai pruning checklist

When the time comes to prune your bonsai, deciding which branch to work on can be overwhelming. These are the general guidelines you will follow; they should make your job a lot easier and get you thinking in the right way about how to create a balanced tree.

Break the rules

These are only general guidelines and you do not have to follow them slavishly. If you think a branch works for a particular tree – even though it might go against this list – then why not try it out?

Understanding the purpose of pruning can help you when shaping your own tree. The species type and what you want it to ultimately look like will likewise determine your approach to pruning. Many bonsai are inspired by nature (see page 116) and following these general guidelines will help you achieve a graceful and natural look.

First place your bonsai at eye level with its front facing you. Every tree has a front – or preferred viewing angle – where it looks its best. This is totally up to you. Next remove any dead branches that make it hard to study your tree, then observe it closely and move the branches around to see where they are really stemming from. This will help you to decide which branches are unnecessary for your design.

Generally, the bottom third of the trunk in most bonsai has no branches.

What to prune

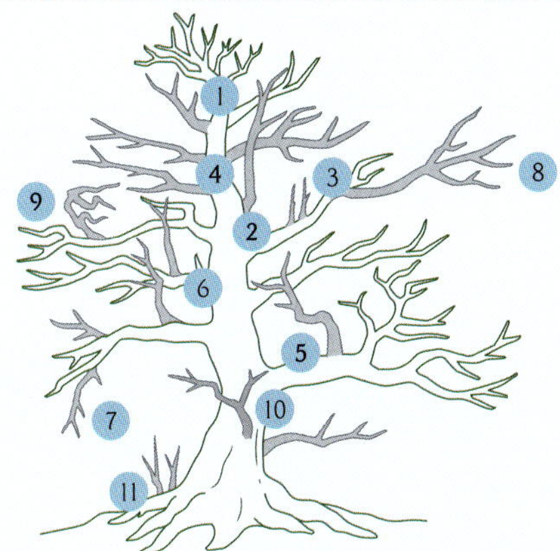

1 Competing trunkline branches (branches the same thickness as the trunk) are removed to keep one dominant trunk and create a natural, mature look.

2 Crossing branches are cut to prevent clutter and visual confusion.

3 Eye-poker branches (branches growing directly towards the viewer) are pruned because they break the silhouette and look aggressive.

4 Handlebar or bar branches (branches growing directly opposite each other, resembling the handlebars on a bicycle) removed to avoid a rigid, artificial feel.

5 Branches growing inwards towards the trunk are cut to improve airflow and reduce congestion.

6 Inner branches growing upwards are removed to maintain a natural branch flow.

7 Dangling growth and hanging branches are trimmed to keep the tree's energy strong and upward flowing.

8 Extra-long shoots are pruned to keep the tree in shape.

9 Unnatural-looking bends in the trunk or branches are corrected to avoid odd, jarring lines.

10 Growth that is too low is removed to reveal the trunk's strength and age.

11 Suckers at the base of the trunk are cut as they can take energy from more important branches.

Above: Before you start pruning a tree stop to consider why and if so doing is necessary.

When not to prune your trees

Pruning is one of the most fun parts of bonsai, but it is important not to get carried away. Knowing when not to is just as important as knowing when to prune.

Pruning at the wrong time can weaken a bonsai and slow its growth; it can even stop it from flowering. Beginners tend to trim new growth too often as a way of trying to keep their trees looking neat all the time, but trees need strong growth phases to stay healthy. If a tree is weak then pruning only adds more stress.

When not to prune a bonsai

Never prune a weak or sick tree.
Cutting off new growth removes its only source of energy production, making it even weaker. Always let the tree recover.

Do not prune if you want a branch to thicken.
Letting a branch grow freely allows it to get thicker. Pruning too early slows down development.

Avoid pruning after repotting.
Trees need time to recover and establish new roots, and pruning the roots and branches at the same time can cause too much stress. If an excessive number of roots have been removed during repotting, it is often a good idea to balance out the foliage to match by removing some unnecessary branches.

Hold off from pruning flowering trees before they bloom.
Many species produce flower buds on last season's growth and pruning too early removes the following year's flowers.

Have a reason for pruning.
Before you reach for the scissors, always ask yourself why you are going to prune. If it is not for health, structure or refinement, then it is best to leave the tree to grow a little longer.

WHAT IS THE TWO-BRANCH PRINCIPLE?

To wire a bonsai, we follow what is known as the two-branch principle, or double wiring. This involves wiring one branch to another so that each branch anchors the wire in place and ensures the wire will hold the branches in the desired position. Here the wiring process is shown on a Nagasaki crabapple (*Malus cerasifera*).

1 **Wire the first branch**
Inspect the branches, then apply the wire to the first branch. Here I am going to wire the branch on the left first (opposite, top left and right).

2 **Anchor the wire**
Bend the wire around the trunk once to anchor it. This ensures that there is no movement of the wire against the bark which would scrape and scar the tree (opposite, centre left).

3 **Using one wire**
Here (opposite, centre right), you can clearly see how two branches were wired with one piece of wire. As you get more practice in this, you can apply this technique to an entire foliage pad on other trees.

4 **Shaping the branches**
Once the branches are wired, you can then manipulate the branches into the desired position and the wire will hold them in place (opposite, bottom). Remember to remove this wire just as it slightly bites into the branch, otherwise it will leave a scar.

Keep things even

When wiring, keep each coil evenly spaced for a cleaner, more effective, result. For better control, hold the branch near the previous coil as you wrap as this helps maintain stability and precision.

Achieving balance: mastering style and composition

Below: A bold and balanced Fuji cherry (*Prunus incisa* 'Kojo-no-mai') positioned in the centre of the composition creates a calm, grounded visual impact, ideal for showcasing symmetry and structure.

The best bonsai tell a story and evoke emotion, much like a painting or photograph. Context and composition are key to this and to changing the visual mood of a tree. It may seem complicated, but once you understand some simple composition theory you will be well on your way to making beautiful and engaging trees.

THE RULE OF THIRDS

The rule of thirds is one of the most well-known compositional guidelines. It is used in photography, painting and even bonsai to divide a piece of art into nine squares using horizontal and vertical lines. The four points where the lines overlap are called the focal points. Placing the parts of the bonsai you want to draw attention to on some (but not all) of the focal points creates a visually engaging composition.

Sometimes, we position a tree dead-centre for a bold, balanced look. Other times, shifting it off-centre creates a more dynamic feel. This is just one of many composition tools, but I find it the most useful.

BRANCH PLACEMENT

One of the biggest mistakes I see beginners make (which isn't a bad thing since we are all learning) is to place branches randomly without taking a step back to see how they all work together. If you look at trees in nature, you will observe how the branches get shorter as they get nearer the apex; empty spaces can create depth, and a strong taper can make a tree look more powerful. Everything should appear to be connected and organic, so if you are styling and you see something that sticks out or looks too out of place, maybe it needs to change.

Above: Placing this *Rhododendron* (Satsuki group) 'Gumpo White' off-centre adds movement and interest. This dynamic composition feels more natural and helps guide the viewer's eye across the visual plane.

Seeking inspiration from nature

To create a bonsai that truly feels natural, simply observe trees in nature. Study how they grow, such as where branches stem from and how they react to their environment. A naturalistic bonsai should not look as though it was styled by a human, but like a miniaturized tree grown without intervention.

UNDERSTANDING NATURAL GROWTH

Too often we can look at so many bonsai that when we style a tree, we are simply mimicking what we have already seen. Go out into nature and take it all in. Observe a tree's trunkline, how it tapers, how its branches flow, its foliage pads (see page 100), ramification (see page 99) and the negative space between the branches. Then when you create a tree, bring to life the aspects of nature that inspire you. Everyone sees the natural world differently, and your bonsai should reflect the beauty that speaks to you. To me, this is what makes bonsai an art, through personal expression, observation and interpretation.

You can take inspiration from a particular species' older self, recreating how it would look in nature, such as an oak bonsai styled to look like an ancient tree standing in the forest. But you can break this rule. Instead of making a tree look like an older representation of itself, why not challenge yourself to style a bonsai after a different species? Nigel Saunders – one of my great inspirations in bonsai – has trained a tree of a thousand stars (*Serissa japonica*) to look like an acacia tree. It is an approach heavily inspired by nature but with a creative twist.

Opposite: This naturalistic bonsai captures the essence of a tree growing in the wild. Its layered branching, uneven spacing, and exposed roots reflect the way trees adapt to their environment over time.

Five outdoor bonsai for shady spots

When you look at trees in nature, you will see that not all outdoor bonsai like full sun. Some species prefer to be in a shaded spot that receives indirect sunlight. These have naturally evolved in the shaded parts of a forest or an environment that does not get much sun. If your garden is shaded, then these trees may be for you.

Trees that like shaded spots can sometimes suffer if they are placed in full sun. Japanese maples (*Acer palmatum*), for example, can easily get leaf burn if they are left too long under the hot midday summer sun. However, they will benefit from full sun in early and mid-spring. A common beginner mistake is assuming that when a tree is classed as needing partial shade, it does not need to be watered as much. While they generally lose less moisture because they are not in direct sunlight, these trees do still need consistent watering to stay healthy.

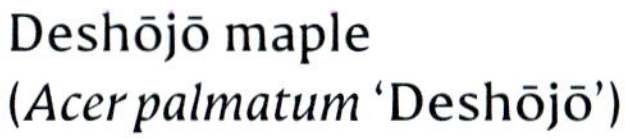

Deshōjō maple (*Acer palmatum* 'Deshōjō')

There are hundreds of varieties of Japanese maple, but this stunning variety is sought after for its bright red foliage that emerges in spring. The leaves then turn a vibrant green before becoming golden orange and fiery red as they come into autumn. As with most maple, the Deshōjō likes some shade and does well under shade netting, or even 30–50 per cent shade cloth (a fabric used to protect plants from too much sun). On very hot days, keep on top of watering since they require consistent moisture levels. In winter keep them between -10°C (14°F) and 5°C (41°F) to ensure they enter dormancy.

Satsuki azalea (*Rhododendron indicum*)

The most popular of all flowering bonsai, the azalea comes in thousands of different varieties with all sorts of colours of flowers and leaf variations. They are the best trees for shaded gardens since they thrive in sheltered spots. This semi-evergreen has delicate oval-shaped leaves and responds well to pruning by back budding from a bare branch (if the tree is in good health). It likes a more acidic soil such as kanuma, or even ericaceous compost mixed with some perlite. I find that a bit of morning sun promotes better flowering, but too much can dry out the foliage. In winter, keep them between -5°C (23°F) and 5°C (41°F) to ensure they become dormant.

Maidenhair tree (*Ginkgo biloba*)

This ancient deciduous species has been on our planet for more than 200 million years, making it a genuine living fossil. It can deal with full sun, but I have found that it does much better in a shaded spot. Too much direct sunlight can dry out its delicate double-lobed fan-shaped leaves. It prefers well-drained soil and needs regular watering during the growing season. In autumn its leaves turn from a light green to a beautiful vibrant yellow before being shed by the tree all in one go. This is known as the great ginkgo leaf dump. In winter, I like to keep mine at temperatures between 10°C (14°F) and 5°C (41°F) to ensure a stable dormancy period.

Cinquefoil (*Potentilla fruticosa*)

Once seen as an unconventional species for bonsai, many artists have begun to train this deciduous shrub with great success. It can get leaf burn in too much sun, and so in the growing season I keep mine in a spot that gets morning sun and afternoon shade. It thrives in a soil that drains well but remember to keep on top of watering, especially on hot days. Depending on the variety, the flowers can be orange, yellow, white or pink. In winter I keep them between -10°C (14°F) and 5°C (41°F) to ensure they stay dormant.

Wilson's honeysuckle (*Lonicera nitida*)

This fantastic fast-growing species is loved for its small green leaves and dense foliage that can easily be trained into pads in a short amount of time. This is also known as the 'hedging honeysuckle' since people often use it in their gardens to create hedges. It is very adaptable to different growing conditions and soil types (honestly it can be a bit of a weed sometimes) but this is what makes it so great for bonsai. It does best in partial shade and can be trimmed multiple times per year. In winter it tolerates temperatures between -10°C (14°F) and 5°C (41°F) as its growth slows and it enters dormancy.

Five more bonsai for gentle light:

- Lady's eardrops (*Fuchsia magellanica*)
- Chinese privet (*Ligustrum sinense*)
- Japanese holly (*Ilex crenata*)
- Silver birch (*Betula pendula*)
- European hornbeam (*Carpinus betulus*)

Repotting with confidence

Repotting is instrumental in keeping your tree healthy and helping its development. Work out how to determine when to repot your bonsai, how to do it safely and how to manage the roots during the process.

Why repotting matters: keeping your bonsai healthy

Over time bonsai roots become compact and tangled and this can reduce the tree's ability to absorb water and nutrients. Repotting allows them to enjoy fresh soil and better drainage, and creates room for new root growth.

Repot later in the year

If necessary, you can also repot single-flush pines in the late summer or early autumn.

Opposite: Sphagnum moss is added around the base of a Wilson's honeysuckle (*Lonicera nitida*) after repotting to retain humidity and protect exposed roots while they recover. Once you see signs of growth on the foliage, the moss can be removed before the roots grow up into the moss.

WHEN TO REPOT

Knowing when to repot is as important as the process itself. The best time for most species is late winter to early spring. Most bonsai need to be repotted every two to five years, but this varies depending on the species, pot size and age of the tree. Signs that your tree needs a repot are that water may not drain out of the drainage holes as quickly as before, the tree may have reduced vigour, its compact root system is encircling the pot or roots are coming out of the drainage holes. For deciduous trees, early spring is when the energy moves into the branches to push out new growth, making it safe to work on the roots. A good indicator that it is time to repot these trees is to look for the moment the buds begin to open.

REMEMBER THE EXCEPTIONS

Not every tree needs the same type of care, and there are exceptions to the rules. Single-flush pines, for example, are best repotted in spring, just as buds swell; but they can also be repotted in late summer or early autumn. Tropical species including *Ficus* are best repotted in early summer when they are actively growing and will recover faster. Always research the species to ensure you are repotting at the right time.

How to repot like a pro

Here's how to perform a basic repot. So doing simply involves untangling the tree's roots, removing any extra-long, thick or upward-growing ones, then putting the tree back into a bonsai pot with fresh soil. A common mistake beginners make is to repot a healthy tree too soon. Always check if your bonsai truly needs repotting before disturbing its roots (see page 124).

1 **Remove the bonsai from the pot**
Carefully take the tree out of the pot. If it won't budge, don't force it, use a spatula tool to loosen the soil around the edges of the pot and then the tree should come out with ease.

2 **Rake the roots**
Use a bamboo or wooden chopstick, a root hook or a root rake (see page 21) to rake out the untangled roots to loosen and remove the soil (above left). Always rake the roots radially out from the trunk so that you do not tear through any you want to keep.

3 **Wash the roots**
This is an optional step and best only done to remove old compacted soil. Do not wash the roots of a pine or conifer since these species rely on beneficial mycorrhizal fungi (a fungi that forms a network from the tree's roots which helps to feed the tree) in the soil that can be disrupted if too much is washed away.

Keep roots damp

When the roots are exposed to air, it's important to prevent them from drying out, especially on hot or windy days. Have a spray bottle of water nearby and mist the roots occasionally to keep them hydrated. Once roots dry out, they're essentially dead, so keeping them hydrated gives you more time to prune.

4 **Profile prune the roots**

Profile pruning involves cutting back a tree's roots, and helps plant health. Sit the tree over the new pot to do this and prune back so there is about 1cm (½in) between the rootball and the inside of the pot for the roots to grow into over the next couple of years. Prune carefully if there are not many roots: you do not want to leave the tree with none at all.

5 **Remove any problem roots**

The goal is to keep the lateral growing roots and remove any roots that are too thick, or that are crossing or growing upwards. Here (above right), I am pruning a root that had hit the side of the pot and begun to curl. If such a root is allowed to grow and thicken it may look unnatural.

6 Choose a new pot

A bonsai's pot is just as important as the tree itself so take care when choosing a new one. I like to place the trees I'm repotting into different pots to see how they look first before making a final selection (see page 132).

7 Prepare the pot

Put some drainage mesh in the base of the pot and secure it with wire (bottom left). So doing ensures that the bonsai soil does not fall through the drainage holes. Feed another length of wire up through the drainage holes (some pots have dedicated wire holes). This will be used to anchor the tree in the pot later on.

8 Add the soil

Make a mountain of soil in the pot so that when you position the tree in it there is no air gap under the root ball (bottom right). Large air pockets create areas where water cannot reach and as a result the roots in that part of the pot can dry up.

9 **Add the tree**

Place the tree in the pot at the desired angle, then add more soil and use a chopstick to gently work out any air gaps (bottom left). Take time to check the planting angle at this stage before you secure the tree.

10 **Anchor the tree**

Once the tree is secure, bring the two ends of the anchoring wire together and twist them to hold the bonsai in place. This will prevent the tree wobbling as new roots form. I have used a piece of an old T-shirt to protect the trunk and *nebari* (see page 130) from being damaged by the wire (bottom right). Once the roots have filled the pot, the anchoring wire can be removed.

11 **Water the tree**

Add water until it runs clear through the drainage holes. Ensure that the water drains freely.

Just add moss

To help keep the humidity levels up, you can place some sphagnum moss on the surface of the soil until you notice new growth on the tree. Remove the moss before the roots start growing upwards and into it.

Root care: developing a beautiful *nebari*

Nebari is the Japanese term for the surface roots in bonsai, and refers to the visible root flare above the soil. A well-developed *nebari* gives a tree visual stability – it's as if the tree is firmly anchored to the ground. Don't worry if your tree does not have a good *nebari*, it can be improved and developed.

The best time to work on *nebari* is during repotting. Each time you repot a bonsai, really take your time and think carefully about your pruning since it may be a few years before you work on the roots again.

You should carefully prune and position the roots. Spread them out radially, removing any downwards, upwards, or crossing roots to encourage a balanced, more natural look (top left). If any roots seem too big and heavy for the others around them, prune them off with some root cutters (top right) or, for larger trees, some loppers (bottom left). Once the fine-feeder roots are positioned radially and evenly spaced, pot the tree and let time do its work (bottom right). These roots will gradually thicken and the *nebari* will get better with each repot. To speed up the process, planting the tree in the ground allows unrestricted root growth, leading to faster development and a stronger root flare.

An even spread

When positioning roots, imagine them as the spokes of a bicycle wheel. Aim to spread them evenly in all directions for a more balanced *nebari* in the future.

PLANTING IN A POND BASKET

I like to plant developing trees in pond baskets to encourage better root growth. Unlike solid pots, pond baskets have holes all around, allowing you to air-prune them. When roots reach the edge of the basket, instead of circling inside the pot they grow through the holes and dry up. This signals to the tree that it needs to send out more lateral roots further inside, promoting finer root division and creating a denser network of feeder roots. This leads to a stronger, more even *nebari* in a shorter period of time. This method is really effective for species that respond well to root pruning such as maples and elms.

Above: A pond basket encourages outwards root growth and prevents circling roots. This helps create stronger *nebari* by promoting even, radial root development and more root density.

Perfect pots: choosing bonsai containers

In bonsai, the pot is as important as the tree. Just as a frame is used to enhance a great painting, the right pot can enhance a tree's shape, style and overall feel. Looks are not the only factor here either. Depending on the species, the depth of the pot also plays a role in your tree's health.

In Japan, conifers are traditionally placed in unglazed pots and deciduous trees are given glazed pots. However, as bonsai has spread across the world innovation has led to exciting new pairings. Do not be afraid to break the rules; create contrasting combinations by placing species such as juniper into boldly coloured pots and delicate flowering species into less elaborate containers. Bonsai is an art, and with any art experimenting can lead to more unique and expressive pieces.

Keep it in proportion

As a general rule when potting a bonsai, for it to look proportional, the height of the pot should be roughly the same as the thickness of the trunk at the base.

VISUAL CHARACTERISTICS TO CONSIDER

The right pot should bring out the best in your tree, not overpower it. The colour of the pot can complement the bark, leaves or flowers to create a harmonious look. A contrasting colour can make other features of a tree stand out. Texture and shape also play a role. A smooth pot with round edges can work well with a delicate tree with flowing lines, while a textured, rectangular aged pot can pair well with a more weathered tree.

COLOUR THEORY FOR BEGINNERS

For the most contrast and 'pop' between a tree and its pot, select complementary colours. These are shades that are opposite each other on the colour wheel. For example, when a Beni-maiko Japanese maple (*Acer palmatum* 'Beni-maiko') bursts into vibrant red foliage in spring, pairing it with a green-glazed pot makes the colour stand out even more.

If you prefer a more natural look, where the tree and pot blend together, go for harmonious colours. These are shades that sit close together on the colour wheel, such as red, orange and yellow. For example, Japanese black pines (*Pinus thunbergii*) have greyish bark, so an unglazed pot in a similar tone can enhance that connection.

Below: These pots show how colour choice can dramatically affect a bonsai's presentation. The muted, dark container on the left provides a natural, grounding base that highlights the strength and structure of a Japanese black pine (*Pinus thunbergii*). The vibrant turquoise pot on the right creates a bold contrast with the red foliage of a Japanese maple (*Acer palmatum*), using complementary colours to make the tree pop visually.

Five stunning bonsai and their ideal containers

Choosing a pot for your bonsai may sound simple, but it involves much more than just picking something that looks nice. A great pot should bring out the best in your tree, complementing its style, shape, colour and texture to create an overall feeling.

These classic species-style bonsai and pot combinations are perfect for beginners, since each tree's natural characteristics lend themselves to the pairing. These examples will help you to develop your skills and give you a strong foundation in bonsai styling.

Darwin's barberry (*Berberis darwinii*) in a pale green round glazed pot

Berberis is an evergreen shrub that has small, rounded spiky leaves. In spring, it bursts with yellow flowers, followed by red berries in autumn when its leaves turn a rusty red. Its fine branches and thorny structure make it look like a miniature holly tree, and these features make it just perfect for bonsai. When you are looking for new and interesting species to try out, those with small leaves are excellent to work with. A shallow, round pale green glazed pot softens this species' spiky leaves, complementing the reds of the leaves and berries.

Chinese quince (*Pseudocydonia sinensis*) in an oval cream glazed pot

The Chinese quince is known for its delicate pink blossoms that emerge in early spring. They are often placed into glazed pots with muted colours to enhance their vibrant blooms. The soft curves of an oval cream pot work with the tree's warm autumn tones and harmonizes with the flowers. I find that softer neutral tones work best because they allow the tree's seasonal transformations – from blossom, to fruit, to golden autumn leaves – to be the focus.

Border forsythia (*Forsythia × intermedia*) in a rectangular dark blue glazed pot

Forsythia is known for its bright yellow flowers that appear right at the start of spring, often emerging before the leaves. When combined with a dark blue glazed rectangular pot, the colour of the pot really complements the vivid yellow blooms, making them pop more. This species lends itself to many bonsai styles and, therefore, the form of the tree will determine the shape of the pot. If it has elegant lines in the trunk and branches, pairing it with a rectangular pot will add visual contrast for an even more striking composition. Forsythia responds well to pruning and back-buds very easily. This is such a rewarding species for beginners to try, however wait until the tree has finished flowering before pruning.

Japanese snowbell (*Styrax japonicus*) in an unglazed brown clay oval pot

The Japanese snowbell is a graceful tree with elegant, arching branches and small, bell-shaped hanging white flowers that emerge in spring. It has smooth greyish bark and a soft branching structure. An unglazed oval brown clay pot pairs beautifully with this tree because it makes the flowers stand out more when they bloom without the composition looking too busy. The oval shape works in harmony with the tree's gentle curves. If you desire a more complementary look, however, you could place it into a cream pot to work in harmony with the white flowers and greyish bark.

Five more stunning bonsai and their ideal containers

- Stewartia (*Stewartia pseudocamellia*) in a rectangular light brown glazed pot
- Japanese larch (*Larix kaempferi*) in a deep round dark brown unglazed pot
- Bougainvillea (*Bougainvillea glabra*) in an oval purple glazed pot
- Sargent juniper (*Juniperus chinensis* var. sargentii) in a rectangular dark brown unglazed pot
- Fukien tea (*Carmona retusa*) in a round deep green glazed pot

Hinoki cypress (*Chamaecyparis obtusa*) in an unglazed red clay rectangular pot

The scale-like foliage of the Hinoki cypress and its naturally upright growth habit make it the perfect subject for an unglazed rectangular pot. Using a pot made from red clay means that its muted red tones will subtly enhance the bonsai's rich green foliage. Since conifers also prefer well-draining soil, the unglazed pot helps absorb excess moisture. This pot and tree combination stays true to traditional Japanese aesthetics, but Hinoki cypress can also look nice in blue glazed pots. Depending on the nature of the tree – whether it has flowing lines or angular movement – you can decide whether you would like the pot to have curved or sharp lines.

Above: Check the roots of a bonsai before repotting it. The roots of this tree have filled the pot and should be repotted. If they look healthy but have not yet filled the pot, return the tree to the pot and allow it to grow for another year.

When you should not repot a bonsai

Knowing when not to repot a bonsai is just as important as repotting itself. Repotting at the wrong time can cause unnecessary stress to a tree and can slow down its development. Before repotting, ask yourself why you are about to do it. This one simple question will help you to avoid repotting mistakes.

Repotting should only be done when necessary and at the correct time of year. As Peter Chan, one of my great inspirations and teachers in bonsai says: 'Why would you cut your stomach open if there is nothing wrong with you?'

When not to repot a bonsai

Never repot a weak or sick tree.
Repotting a tree that is struggling can easily kill it (unless the soil is overly compacted or the roots are rotting, in which case repotting is essential). By doing this, you are just increasing the stress the tree is already under. Let it recover and become healthy before repotting it.

Do not repot in the wrong season.
Most bonsai should be repotted in early spring. However there are some exceptions to this rule – always check the specific species to ensure it is the right time for repotting.

Do not repot during extreme weather.
Repotting during a heatwave or too early in the year, when there is the chance of temperatures dropping again, can cause serious damage.

Avoid repotting a tree that was recently repotted.
Repotting the same tree too soon after a repot can add more stress to a tree that is putting energy into trying to recover from just being moved. Repot every two to five years depending on the age and species.

Only repot when the roots have nowhere else to go.
If there is still room for roots to grow and the soil is draining well then there is no need for a repot just yet.

Right: This Chinese elm (*Ulmus parvifolia*) is being repotted into a more free-draining soil mix.

Growing and creating bonsai

You can propagate your own trees from seeds and cuttings, by air layering and even from a seedling found in the wild. Creating bonsai from scratch gives you more control over the design process from the outset.

From seed to tree:
Patience pays off

Growing a bonsai from seed gives you more control over the style of your bonsai. Genetic variation can also give you more unique trees. It's best to grow from seed alongside regular bonsai practice because it can be years before some species can be worked on. That way, you're still improving your skills while your seedlings develop.

Seed success

Make sure your seeds come from a reliable source to ensure that they are fresh or, better yet, collect your own seeds from your garden or a local park.

1 Pre-soaking the seeds

Whether you have collected or bought them, seeds have usually lost some of their moisture, making them become dormant. Before you stratify seeds (see below), you need to soak them in warm water (make sure it's not too hot) to rehydrate them (opposite, top right). This also helps to soften the protective outer shell and will allow the seeds to germinate more easily.

2 Stratification and germination

Some seeds need to be stratified before they germinate – they must experience a cold, damp period before they will sprout. Stratification mimics winter conditions and encourages seeds to germinate. Place the seeds inside a piece of wet paper towel, then put the towel into a plastic sandwich bag and refrigerate for several weeks or months (how long depends on the species) (opposite, bottom). You can also try natural stratification by planting your seeds outside in autumn; they should germinate come spring.

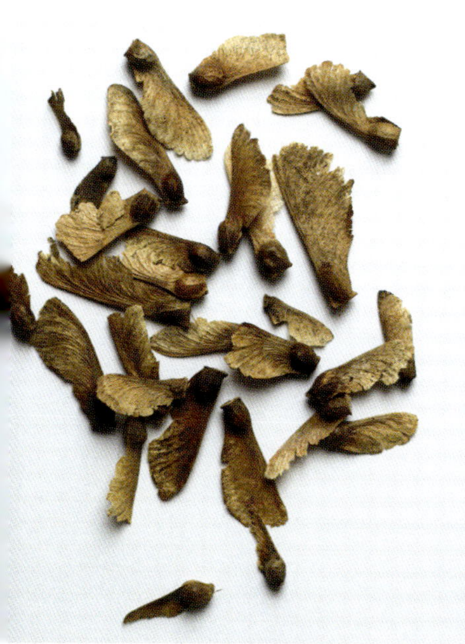

3 Sowing the seeds

When you can see little shoots coming from the seeds they have begun to germinate. Now you can sow them into a seed tray filled with a suitable soil (opposite, top right). I like to use inorganic soil to avoid any fungal problems that could cause issues for the young seedlings. Plant the seed as deep as it is large – but not too deep or it may not make it.

4 Disinfection

This step is optional, and you may think that it is slight overkill, but once I have planted seeds I like to water the soil with a dilute solution of hydrogen peroxide to remove any fungal spores to further improve my success rate. Simply mix 10ml (⅓fl oz) of 3 per cent hydrogen peroxide into 1 litre (1¾ pints) of water. This is strong enough to reduce the fungal spores without harming the seeds.

The correct vintage

Ensure your seeds are fresh and collected within the same year you want to plant them for better success.

5 Aftercare

In the spring, once the seeds have grown, it is important to make sure they continue to develop and stay healthy. I like to spray them with insecticidal soap to protect the delicate shoots from pests. Gently brushing your hand over the seedlings, or gradually exposing them to the wind, helps them to develop stronger trunks by stimulating lignin (an organic material that is the chief constituent of wood) production (opposite, bottom).

6 Development as a bonsai

Once the seedlings are strong, you can separate them out into individual pots and allow their roots to fill the pot as they get bigger. Within one to five years, depending on the size of the trees you are aiming for, you can begin training them as bonsai.

Five bonsai that grow fast from seed

Growing bonsai from seed takes great patience and you may not even see the finished tree in your lifetime. However, some species develop much faster than others and you can see good progress in just a few years if they are given the right care.

If you are just starting to grow plants from seed, I highly recommend these species since they are fast growing and will make your experience much more rewarding. Some of them can develop thick trunks relatively quickly – in just a few years – especially if they are incrementally up-potted or even planted directly into the ground to accelerate their growth. When selecting a species, tropical and deciduous species tend to grow the fastest, while evergreens take a little longer. The key is to provide good care so that you have strong growth right from the start.

Japanese black pine (*Pinus thunbergii*)
This is probably the fastest species to grow from seed to finished bonsai. Its trunk thickens relatively quickly, especially when it is planted in the ground. As a double-flush species, Japanese black pine responds well to pruning and can produce a second flush of growth within a single season, which means even more progress in a shorter time. The tree's craggy bark develops early, making it look aged early on. Its vigorous root system allows for more aggressive root pruning and wiring which further allows you to progress the tree quickly. A great trick to accelerate trunk thickening is to wire young seedlings and allow the wire to bite in deeply, creating a unique texture as the tree swallows the wire over time.

Irish oak (*Quercus petraea*)
One of my favourite oaks for bonsai, the Irish oak is also known as the sessile oak. It germinates easily from collected acorns and grows relatively fast into a tree that can be worked on for bonsai in as little as one or two years. I find that this tree has a more upright growth habit with slightly smaller leaves than other oaks which makes it easier to achieve good proportions in bonsai form. Over time it develops a rugged bark which gives the tree an ancient look, reminiscent of the gnarled old oaks found in the Wicklow Mountains of Ireland.

Flame tree (*Delonix regia*)

Also known as the royal poinciana, the flame tree is a tropical species that makes a fabulous bonsai. It has delicate, fern-like leaves that fold up at night, similar to the Brazilian rain tree (*Pithecellobium tortum*). My favourite feature of this species is its vibrant red flowers, which cover the entire tree in summer, making it look as if it's on fire. It grows quickly from seed, and in my experience germination takes only two to three weeks. It responds well to pruning and can be wired early to create an interesting trunk as it matures.

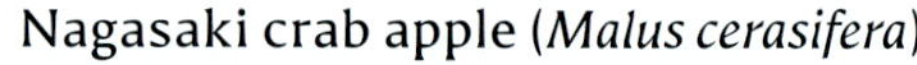

Nagasaki crab apple (*Malus cerasifera*)

A beautiful deciduous species, the Nagasaki crab apple is prized for its gentle pinkish-white flowers that emerge in spring, and the small ornate mini apples that arrive in autumn. Under the right conditions it grows relatively fast from seed. Unlike many other fruit trees that can take many years to bloom, this species can begin to produce flowers in just a few years. If you don't want to wait long to see your bonsai flowering, this is a great choice. Just be sure to give it plenty of sunlight and let it grow unchecked for a thicker trunk in a faster time before using bonsai techniques.

Five more bonsai that grow fast from seed

- Willow-leaf fig (*Ficus salicaria*)
- Golden rain tree (*Koelreuteria paniculata*)
- Swamp cypress (*Taxodium distichum*)
- African baobab (*Adansonia digitata*)
- Japanese apricot (*Prunus mume*)

Trident maple (*Acer buergerianum*)

The trident maple is one of the fastest-growing Japanese maples. It is an excellent choice for beginners to grow from seed. It thickens quickly and, once the trunk reaches the desired size, it responds incredibly well to pruning with fine ramification (see page 99) and dense back-budding. It also tolerates aggressive root pruning in spring, allowing for faster *nebari* (see page 130) development. With its rapid growth, stunning three-lobed leaves and vibrant autumn colours, it's a rewarding species that gives you results much faster than other maples.

Easy propagation:

How to grow bonsai from cuttings

Growing bonsai from cuttings is an easy and cheap way to propagate a tree. It simply involves cutting a branch off a parent tree and using it to create a new one – here I am using a Lawson cypress (*Chamaecyparis lawsoniana*). Choose smaller branches from the last one or two years of growth (larger branches generally have a lower success rate). Make sure the species you want to propagate is suitable for this technique.

Heel or nodal?

If you're working with a species that roots easily, nodal cuttings are fast and easy to do. If the plant is more resistant to rooting, heel cuttings might be worth the extra effort. You can research the species of tree you are working on, but I recommend trying both methods to determine which is best for you.

1 **Decide on the soil type**
Soil type is crucial for a balance of water and aeration. For the majority of cuttings, I recommend 100 per cent perlite. If you find this becomes dry too soon, the standard bonsai soil mix of equal parts pumice, akadama and lava rock (1:1:1) (see page 72) is a good option. Do not add any compost because this may inadvertently introduce fungal problems.

2 **Taking the cutting**
For most bonsai, the best time to take cuttings is in summer, just after the leaves harden on broadleaf trees or during active growth for conifers. Select a young, long, healthy branch that has lignified (become woody) since green fleshy branches are less likely to root (opposite, top).

3 **Types of cutting**
There are two types of cuttings. Heel cuttings (opposite, bottom left) are torn from a larger branch, leaving a 'heel' that is then cut clean. Nodal cuttings (opposite, bottom right) are made just below a node. Both methods target areas rich in growth hormones, enhancing propagation success. The tree in the bottom right image is a Hinoki cypress (*Chamaecyparis obtusa* 'Nana Gracilis').

4 Preparing the cutting

For the best results, plant the cutting half the depth as the cutting is long. So doing ensures that it remains stable while the delicate new roots form. Remove any foliage from the bottom half of the cutting before planting since this will not get any light and will rot under the soil which could hinder root development (opposite, top left).

5 Use a rooting hormone

A rooting hormone with the active ingredient IBA (indole-3-butyric acid) greatly increases your chances of success because it mimics the growth hormone auxin that is responsible for root growth and allows the cuttings to root at a much faster rate. You can buy it is as a powder or gel and simply dip the base of the cutting into it (opposite, top right).

6 Planting the cutting

Choose a pot which is twice as deep as the cutting will be planted. Make a pilot hole with a chopstick, then insert the cutting and push down on the soil around it to secure it (opposite, bottom). You can plant multiple cuttings in a pot. To keep humidity levels high, create a mini greenhouse by placing the pot in a clear plastic bag. Take it out of the bag once a week to prevent fungi from forming. Keep it in a warm place until new roots form – check once a month for new root growth. The time it takes a cutting to root depends on the species; for example, a Chinese elm (*Ulmus parvifolia*) will root in as little as three to six weeks whereas some junipers take twelve to eighteen months. The trees here are Chinese juniper 'Itoigawa' (*Juniperus chinensis* 'Itoigawa').

Further development

Once your cuttings have taken root, separate them out into slightly larger individual pots in which they can grow and thicken in the coming years. They can then be trained into future bonsai.

Air layering:
a magic trick for new growth

Air layering is one of the best ways to propagate trees for bonsai. Not only do you produce a tree that is genetically identical to its parent, but you can use much thicker branches from other larger trees, which gives you a head start in terms of development. This technique involves making new roots from a trunk or branch by cutting off the nutrients from the existing root system. The section of tree with the new roots is then removed from the original tree and grown separately.

1 Select your air layer

Choose a healthy, vigorous branch or trunk section with good movement and taper, one that you can visualize as a standalone bonsai. Here I am using an apple (*Malus*) tree. Ensure there is plenty of foliage on top so that it can stay healthy while roots develop (opposite, top left). This is best done in the summer or, in climates with shorter growing seasons, in early spring.

2 Cut the trunk

Using a sharp grafting knife, cut a ring of bark below the area you wish to use to form the future *nebari* (opposite, top right). The width of the cut should match the thickness of the branch or trunk you are cutting. Ensure the top cut is clean and even to promote strong root formation.

3 Remove the cambium

When you cut into the trunk it is crucial that you remove all of the cambium – the thin white layer under the bark (opposite, bottom left). If it isn't fully removed, the air layer may fail to develop roots properly because the tissue will rebridge (opposite, bottom right).

Every species is different

Depending on the species, you may need to keep a strip of bark to retain a connection between the top and bottom half of the tree. Easily air-layered species such as apple and maple can be completely ringed, but pines and other conifers do not respond well to the bark being removed completely. Leaving a thin strip of bark allows some water and nutrients through to the rest of the plant.

4 Apply rooting hormone

The roots will emerge above the cut and so next dust a rooting hormone powder containing 0.25 per cent IBA (Indole-3-butyric acid) above it (opposite, top left). The hormone stimulates root growth and speeds up the process. Without it, the tree may still root but it will take longer and may not be as successful.

5 Wrap with sphagnum moss

Soak some sphagnum moss in water and squeeze out the excess moisture. Wrap the moss around the cut section ensuring good contact with the exposed wood (opposite, top right), then wrap the moss ball in plastic wrap or a plastic bag (opposite, bottom left) and seal the top and bottom with aluminium wire to keep the moisture in (opposite, bottom right and below).

Research is key

Not all trees respond well to air layering so research your species before you begin. Online bonsai forums are a great resource, just search for your tree species and the words 'air layering'. This will give you real-world feedback on what works and what doesn't. Trusted horticultural websites, adult education courses at universities, or even arboretum sites also provide propagation advice that is often scientifically backed and comes with step-by-step instructions.

6 Develop roots

Check the moss periodically to make sure it is moist but not soaking wet. Depending on the species, roots can take weeks to months to develop. Apple trees like the one shown here can root in as little as two to three months, Japanese maples take up to three to five months, and conifers such as junipers and pines can take one to two years. Only separate the air layer once there are strong, visible roots throughout the moss (if you use clear plastic it will be a lot easier to see if they have developed). Wrapping the area in aluminium foil or bubble wrap to keep the root ball slightly warm makes the roots develop faster.

7 Separate the new bonsai

Once there are plenty of roots you can cut the air layer off the parent tree (opposite, top left). Handle it carefully to avoid damaging the fragile roots and keep it in a humid environment after separation. Gently remove most of the sphagnum moss so the new roots can develop into the bonsai soil without getting tangled in the moss, which will cause problems later on.

8 Pot the new bonsai

Plant the newly separated tree into a pond basket or training pot with free-draining bonsai soil (see page 70), then water it well and place in a sheltered area to recover (opposite, top right). It is best to allow the new tree to develop a strong, healthy root system (opposite, bottom) before you do any styling and so avoid working on it within the first one or two years.

Above: A young red oak (*Quercus rubra*) sapling growing in the wild. Trees like this can become future bonsai when carefully collected and trained.

Opposite:

Top: A young Japanese black pine (*Pinus thunbergii*) seedling beginning its journey towards becoming a bonsai.

Bottom: A one-year-old dwarf white spruce (*Picea glauca*) seedling. This is a fun choice for beginners exploring bonsai.

Garden to model tree: transforming nursery and collected trees

Starting with some nursery stock, or even trees that have been collected from nature, is a great way to create a bonsai. With material like this time has already done a lot of the work for you, the trunk will have a lot of visual interest and all you need to do is build on the existing branch structure and ramification (see page 99).

When selecting a new tree for bonsai, look out for a tree that has good potential. Pick it up and analyse the trunk and branches, then visualize how you might want it to look. The goal is to envision how the tree will appear once you have refined it.

STARTING WITH NURSERY MATERIAL

Buying an established tree is ideal if you want to start styling right away. Nursery trees, or even trees from a garden centre, are a good place to start because they already have an established root system and a thick trunk. If you are new to bonsai, I recommend practising techniques on an inexpensive bonsai from a garden centre until you get your bearings.

COLLECTING TREES FROM NATURE (*YAMADORI*)

Yamadori – trees collected from the wild – often have incredible character and movement that simply cannot be replicated by humans. This is nature at its finest. Look for examples that display visual age, strong taper and interesting trunk movement. Species such as juniper, pine and deciduous trees with twisted trunks often make exceptional bonsai. However, not every tree is suitable. If a tree is too deeply rooted in a rock or crevice, attempting to remove it may cause fatal damage. In this case, leave it behind and keep searching. I highly recommend collecting with someone experienced in *yamadori* to ensure you are digging up trees correctly and ethically. After collecting and potting the tree, let it recover for two years before carrying out any major styling to ensure its survival and long-term health.

Keep it ethical

In the UK it is illegal to dig up any plant, including algae, lichens and fungi, without the permission of the landowner. If you do have permission to remove a tree, make sure it will survive being transplanted. Plus collecting at the right time of year is also crucial; late winter to early spring is best.

The first styling

Once you know that your collected or nursery tree is in good health, it is time for its first styling. The goal is to set the foundation for future refinement. Here I am using Wilson's honeysuckle (*Lonicera nitida*).

1 Study the tree

Observe the tree from every angle. Identify the side that will be the front, check for movement in the trunk and look for any interesting features such as deadwood or a strong taper that you would like to show off. Doing so will make your pruning decisions a lot easier.

2 Pruning

Select the primary branches that will form the future design. Remove any unnecessary branches that do not fit the tree's character or may cause problems in the future (see pages 106–7). Don't over-prune a tree. If you are unsure, you can always keep a branch and decide what to do with it later, when the tree is strong again.

3 Wiring

Now it's time to wire and shape the tree. Start with the thickest branches and work your way through to the finer ones. Take your time and take care not to snap a branch, especially on trees collected from nature since they may have more brittle wood (opposite, top left).

Keep a record

Take lots of photos to track the progression of your trees. Bonsai is a slow and ongoing process and looking back to where your tree started will show you how far it has come.

4 Setting the apex

Choose or create an apex that flows naturally with the tree's movement. To do this, simply take the uppermost side branch and wire it upwards (above right). This will become the new apex and add taper to the trunk. Alternatively, you might embrace a more unconventional apex placement by creating a cascade-style bonsai or even having a deadwood apex (see page 169) that is preserved as a remnant of the original.

5 Aftercare

After styling, the tree will need time to recover. Water it well and keep it out of extreme weather. Avoid additional stress including repotting or heavy pruning for at least a season. The tree will grow again and gradually, over time, you can slowly improve its structure with every styling.

Five bonsai from everyday finds

Not every bonsai has to come from the mountains or a specialist nursery. Sometimes, great bonsai material is growing in your own backyard, whether it's a garden tree, a neglected hedge plant or even a little seedling growing on the side of a path. These have been nicknamed 'urbandori' and can be transformed into incredible bonsai with a bit of patience and vision. And best of all, they are free!

Sometimes the best bonsai material is hiding in plain sight. Maybe a garden tree has outgrown its space, or renovations in your outside space mean a tree needs to be removed. Instead of throwing it away, why not make it into a bonsai? Unlike nursery-grown trees, garden trees have endured years of environmental stress, creating unique trunk movement, weathered bark and natural character. In my opinion, these trees often have more character than ones that were mass-produced by a nursery.

Garden privet (*Ligustrum ovalifolium*)

A fantastic choice for bonsai, this privet is commonly found in gardens and garden centres as a hedge plant. It grows quickly, back-buds easily and tolerates heavy pruning, making it perfect for beginners. Its small, green, oval-shaped leaves naturally reduce in size with training, and with regular pruning you can develop a dense, refined canopy in a short time. In summer, it produces clusters of delicate white flowers with a beautiful fragrance that smells just like the taste of Pink Lady apples.

Common hawthorn (*Crataegus monogyna*)

This is a relatively inexpensive and easy-to-find species that commonly grows in gardens. Hawthorn is loved for its gnarled bark, small leaves and beautiful flowers that emerge in spring and are followed by little red berries in autumn. It tolerates hard pruning which makes it very easy to shape using the clip-and-grow technique (see page 93). With enough patience you can create a beautiful tree that has a natural look with fine ramification (see page 99). The key is to find a good piece of raw material to build on.

Irish ivy (*Hedera hibernica*)

An unusual but very interesting species to create a bonsai from, ivy can be a nuisance in a garden if it is unwanted. If you are digging some up, why not put it into a pot and develop it as a bonsai? Its naturally small leaves and contorted trunk with rapid growth make it an excellent subject for bonsai. It thrives with regular pruning and back-buds well to create a dense structure over time. If you are more creative, you can even incorporate its aerial roots to give it a more mysterious look, like old forest ruins.

Narrow-leaved mock privet (*Phillyrea angustifolia*)

This is a slightly less common bonsai species, but a fantastic one to work with. Phillyrea is a Mediterranean evergreen, closely related to the olive. The tree has small, narrow leaves that are perfect for compact foliage pads and, with age, it develops beautifully flaky bark. It responds well to pruning and back-buds easily, making it straightforward to keep tidy and dense. Phillyrea thrives in full sun and prefers a free-draining soil mix. Just be sure to keep on top of the watering during hot weather, as it can dry out quickly.

Five more bonsai from everyday finds

- Sweet gum (*Liquidambar styraciflua*)
- Horse chestnut (*Aesculus hippocastanum*)
- European ash (*Fraxinus excelsior*)
- Rosemary (*Salvia rosmarinus*)
- Chinese or Japanese wisteria (*Wisteria sinensis* or *floribunda*)

Small-leaved fuchsia (*Fuchsia microphylla*)

It may be an unconventional species, but fuchsia is an excellent subject for bonsai. It has naturally small leaves and beautiful pendulous flowers that bloom from late spring to early autumn. The plants are super easy to find in garden centres and are popular in household gardens. I have found that the branches can snap easily, therefore I recommend sticking to clip-and-grow with this species. It thrives in moist conditions and benefits from a slightly more retentive soil mix. I plant them in a mix of equal parts compost and perlite.

Taking it up a notch: creating a *tanuki* bonsai

Now that you have learned some basic bonsai techniques, why not try something a little more advanced? One of the most rewarding projects you can tackle is creating a *tanuki* bonsai, sometimes referred to as the 'phoenix graft'. It involves combining living material with a beautiful piece of deadwood to create the illusion of a much older tree.

Tanuki are raccoon dogs which live in some mountainous regions of Japan. The name also refers to mythical creatures depicted as shapeshifting raccoon dogs. These *tanuki* are known for their trickery and illusion, and in the same way that a *tanuki* tricks a person, a *tanuki* bonsai pretends to be much older and more majestic than it really is. Some may consider this as cheating, but if it is done well it can be a creative technique that will give you beautiful results in a much shorter time.

Telling the truth

The reason that *tanuki* are considered as 'cheating' is because they are meant to mimic the look of true *yamadori* (trees collected from nature), which can often sell for millions of yen. There were cases in Japan of fake *yamadori* (*tanuki*) being sold as the real thing, only to be discovered later as fraudulent.

Opposite: A dramatic *tanuki* bonsai combines a twisting shimpaku juniper (*Juniperus chinensis* 'Shimpaku') with striking deadwood to mimic the age and character of an ancient tree.

Right: The living trunk of a shimpaku juniper is fixed into a groove carved into the deadwood, creating a seamless and natural-looking fusion.

Above: A Chinese juniper 'Itoigawa' (*Juniperus chinensis* 'itoigawa'). The live vein has twisted around a beautiful piece of deadwood and fused into it over time to create the illusion of age by combining live growth with an old, weathered trunk.

CREATING A TANUKI

To create a *tanuki* bonsai, you will need a piece of hardwood deadwood with lots of movement and texture. The more gnarled the deadwood, the better. Use wood-carving tools to create a shallow groove that runs along the surface of the deadwood, working in the direction of the natural grain so that the finished tree looks more realistic. While you can use any species, junipers are the most popular for this as the live trees often have areas of deadwood, and they have flexible trunks. Choose a young tree and sit it carefully into the groove. Secure it in place with wire or cable ties, making sure it sits snugly inside the carved channel. Over time, the tree will thicken and wedge itself into the deadwood, and combine with it naturally. If this is done well, the join can become almost invisible.

CHOOSING THE RIGHT PIECE OF DEADWOOD

When creating your *tanuki*, the deadwood is just as important as the living tree to which you join it. Find a piece that is already well-aged. I like to use Irish bogwood, a form of wood that has been preserved in peat bogs, sometimes for thousands of years. Alternatively you can give a second life to driftwood from the beach or even repurpose a bonsai that has died – just make sure the wood is completely dry and rot-free before you start working with it. Since the wood is no longer in the environment that naturally preserved it, just like a *jin*, *shari* and *uro* (see page 175), it's important to apply lime sulphur once a year to help protect the deadwood and keep it looking clean and well-maintained (see page 175).

Above left: A shimpaku juniper (*Juniperus chinensis* 'Shimpaku') styled as a *tanuki* bonsai. The live trunk is skillfully integrated into an expressive piece of driftwood.

Above: This tray-planted, dwarfed *tanuki* composition reflects the Japanese and East Asian art of combining living trees with deadwood to evoke the illusion of ancient natural beauty.

Adding drama: deadwood features and ancient aesthetics

Deadwood can be an excellent feature to add to a tree if you want to create a sense of age and tell a story. Techniques such as making a *shari*, *jin* and *uro* can create the illusion of time, suggesting that a tree may have survived the harshest conditions. At first this method might feel too specialist to try, but once you get the hang of it you will have another skill you can use to further enhance your bonsai.

The most captivating bonsai often tell a story of survival. Perhaps a tree was struck by lightning or has endured terrible storms. A deadwood feature is a testament to a tree's resilience, with a live vein running through it. Some species naturally lend themselves to these features. Junipers work well since they are more rot-resistant, while mountain pines such as Scots pine (*Pinus sylvestris)* and Japanese black pine (*Pinus thunbergii*) develop striking deadwood through exposure to harsh conditions. Even deciduous trees can form beautiful *uro* (see page 175) when old branches die back. These features naturally occur in the wild so there's no reason not to replicate them. Before considering deadwood, ask yourself why you want to use it. It's easy to add features for the sake of it, rather than to enhance the character and value of the tree itself.

Opposite: This mugo pine (*Pinus mugo*) features a striking *shari* that runs elegantly down one side of the trunk, flowing naturally into aged *jins* for a cohesive and timeless appearance.

Take care

Be sure to take all the necessary safety precautions when using rotary tools and chemicals.

SHARI

The deadwood along the trunk of a bonsai is called *shari*. It can be created by removing sections of bark to reveal the wood underneath. Before doing this, use chalk to mark out where you will cut. This ensures that you do not 'ring' the tree, which is what happens when a complete strip of bark is removed all the way around the tree and cuts off the connection between the top and bottom of the tree. Then use a grafting knife or carving tool to cut away the bark in the desired area. The key to a realistic *shari* is to create natural-looking lines that follow the movement of the trunk.

JIN

A *jin* is a branch that has had the bark stripped off to expose the wood underneath. It is a common feature in juniper and pines and gives the impression of strong winds battering the tree, or heavy snow causing the branches to snap off. To make a *jin* from a live branch, start by removing the foliage so that it is bare. Then, use *jin* pliers to squeeze the branch to separate the bark from the wood and allow it to peel off easily. Ensure that you have cut a point at the bottom of the branch so that the *jin* does not continue to tear down the trunk to parts of your tree you didn't want to touch.

URO

One of the main features of a *sabamiki*-style bonsai (see page 25), an *uro* is the hollow at the base of the trunk. It is more common in deciduous species since their wood tends to rot a lot faster and so is seen more often on these species in the wild. *Uro* can be tricky at first, but once you get the hang of the technique it is straightforward. To make a hollow I use a rotary tool fitted with a router bit to carve out sections of the trunk. When carving, try to make the hollow look organic to accurately replicate what nature does best. Try to avoid leaving tool marks or perfectly round hollows since these can look unnatural.

Preserving deadwood

If left untreated, deadwood will eventually rot. To stop this, use lime sulphur to preserve and whiten it to create a striking contrast (a thin layer of calcium sulphate will form as it oxidizes). I use full-strength lime sulphur because it is more effective. After creating a *shari* or *jin*, allow the exposed wood to dry and age naturally for one or two years before application. The lime sulphur will make an *uro* feature too white which can look unnatural. I mix black Indian ink with the lime sulphur to preserve and darken the hollow.

Opposite: A dramatic Chinese juniper 'Itoigawa' (*Juniperus chinensis* 'Itoigawa') bonsai displaying expertly carved *shari* and *jin* features. The flowing deadwood highlights the tree's movement and age.

Moss: ground cover with purpose

In bonsai, moss can be a good and a bad thing. It looks beautiful, giving the impression of a tree that has been untouched for years, and aids moisture retention. But it can attract pests and smother roots. Once you know when and how to use it effectively, you can ensure that your trees stay happy while enhancing them.

ADDING MOSS TO YOUR TREES

It is pretty easy to add moss to your bonsai: you can either wait for it to develop by introducing moss spores, or you can use some that you have collected, from places such as your garden path or wall. Use a wallpaper scraper to remove it in bigger, easier-to-manage pieces, then simply lay it carefully on the surface of the soil and, in a few weeks, it will embed itself into the soil and become a natural part of your bonsai.

PREVENTING PROBLEMS

Moss will protect the surface roots of a bonsai and help retain moisture levels in the soil, especially on hot days. However, it does come with its drawbacks. If it grows too long and thick, it can hold too much moisture which may lead to root rot and fungal issues in the soil. To prevent this, thin out and trim the moss to keep it in check. Moss can also attract birds that will steal it for their nests. If they peck at the bonsai's roots they may stress the tree or leave scars. If birds are persistent, move your bonsai to a more sheltered location.

Opposite

Top: Moss is carefully applied to the bonsai surface to create a natural woodland effect.

Bottom left and right: Moss not only enhances the tree's visual appeal but also helps retain moisture around the roots.

How to beat pests and problems

Pests and fungal issues can affect any tree so knowing what to look out for and how to treat problems is essential. Regular checks such as weeding, rotating your trees, tool hygiene and wound care will keep your bonsai well-maintained and ensure that you stay on top of any issues.

Uninvited guests: how to handle pests

No matter how well you care for your bonsai and keep them healthy, pests can still find a way in.

On large trees, pests such as aphids and scale insects usually aren't a big issue because the tree has plenty of resources to help it to recover from any attacks. But for small trees in pots, where every bit of energy matters, pests can quickly weaken the tree if left unchecked. The key is to catch them early. Here are some of the most common insects you will face, along with advice on how to identify and deal with them.

APHIDS

The most common insect you will face, aphids can be a range of colours, including green, red, yellow, white and black. They tend to appear in spring, often covering the new foliage as it begins to emerge. Aphids feed by sucking sap from the leaves and stems and this can cause yellowing and distorted growth. They also excrete a sticky substance called honeydew which can lead to the development of sooty mould. If left untreated, they can multiply quickly and overwhelm your tree. You can use a diluted dish soap solution or neem oil to remove them, or introduce natural predators such as ladybirds, which are sometimes available from garden centres during the growing season. Alternatively use a deltamethrin-based insecticide.

VINE WEEVILS

Vine weevils are the most destructive pests. The adult black, pear-shaped beetles chew notches in leaves, but the real danger comes from their larvae which burrow into the soil and feed on the roots. This can greatly damage a tree, and in some cases it can be fatal. The legless larvae are white with brown heads and can sometimes be found when you repot a tree. If you spot adult vine weevils, there's a high chance their larvae are already in the soil. To deal with them, use biological controls such as nematodes, which target the larvae. Or use a systemic insecticide such as acetamiprid. When watered into the soil, it's absorbed by the roots and circulates throughout the tree, killing the larvae as they feed.

SPIDER MITES

At less than 1mm in size, spider mites are extremely difficult to spot. You can confirm their presence by tapping the branches of your trees over a piece of white paper. If the specs that land on the page move or smear, you likely have mites. The more obvious sign is the damage they cause – mites suck the sap from the leaves and leave behind little yellow speckles. If they are not dealt with quickly you may end up dealing with a full infestation. If you suspect a spider-mite infestation, spray thoroughly with a diluted neem-oil solution or insecticidal soap once a week for three to four weeks. Rotating treatments and maintaining good humidity can help disrupt their lifecycle and prevent resistance.

MEALY BUGS

Looking like little clumps of cottonwool, mealy bugs hide in leaf axils (the places where leaves develop) and little cracks and crevices in the bark. They suck the sap from a tree, greatly weakening it and leading to yellowing leaves. Just like aphids, they also excrete honeydew which leads to sooty mould. These bugs can be treated by misting them with isopropyl alcohol (surgical spirit) and wiping them off with a cloth. Neem oil or horticultural oil can also be used to suffocate the pests. As with all pests, it is best to isolate affected trees so that the infestation does not spread to others nearby.

SCALE INSECTS

These often go unnoticed as they can disguise themselves on the bark of your tree. They look like small, grey/white dome-shaped bumps along the branches and trunk. Scale insects attach themselves and suck sap from the tree but, unlike aphids, they have a hard outer shell that protects them from many treatments. I have found that the best way to get rid of them is to dip a toothbrush into some isopropyl alcohol and scrub them away. If there are many of them you can also smother them with horticultural oil.

Take care

Chemical insecticides, can harm bees, birds and your pets so avoid using them if you can. If there is no alternative, check the label for any safety precautions.

Fungal problems

Fungi can be a good and a bad thing. Pines, for example, have a symbiotic relationship with mycorrhizal fungi in the soil, which benefits their health. But other types can cause problems. Some create cosmetic issues, but others can weaken or even kill a tree. Here's what to look out for and the treatment needed.

POWDERY MILDEW

This looks like a thin, white powdery coating on the leaves and it thrives in a warm, humid environment with poor airflow. It can lead to leaf drop if untreated. To treat it, remove any infected leaves, spray the tree with a sulphur-based fungicide and move the tree to a place with better airflow.

LEAF BLACK SPOT

As the name suggests, this appears as black or dark brown spots on the leaves. It thrives in warm, wet weather and can spread very fast. Cut off any infected leaves, spray the bonsai with a copper-based fungicide, and move it to improve the airflow around it.

SOOTY MOULD

A black powdery coating on the leaves, sooty mould grows on honeydew secreted by aphids and mealy bugs. It does not harm the bonsai, but it can filter the sunlight which means the leaves will not photosynthesize so well. Control the pests that cause this mould (see page 180), then wipe it off with a damp cloth.

PEACH LEAF CURL

Common in fruit trees such as peach and apricot, this fungus enters the tree during the dormant season. When the leaves emerge in spring, they appear to have red blisters before dropping off. A second flush of leaves usually follows this, and most trees recover from the fungus. For prevention, treat your bonsai with a copper-based fungicide in late winter before any growth starts.

PINE NEEDLE CAST

This causes the needles of pine trees to turn yellow and then brown before they eventually fall off. A tell-tale sign is black lines or spots on the needles before they drop. This fungus can weaken a tree significantly and, if left untreated, can result in its death, especially if it is infected over successive seasons. Pine needle cast thrives in damp environments with poor airflow. Remove and burn any infected needles and treat your pines with a copper-based fungicide. I mist my pines with this fungicide in spring as a preventative measure.

RUST INFECTIONS

Rust fungi appear as orange, yellow or brown pustules on the underside of leaves. These are spores that can spread fast and weaken your tree if not treated. Remove affected leaves, burn them and apply a natural fungicide such as neem oil or sodium bicarbonate solution (made by dissolving 1 teaspoon of bicarbonate of soda in 1 litre/1¾ pints of water). Repeat the treatment once a week until no further signs of infection are visible.

Keep it clean

Always disinfect your tools between working on each tree to prevent the spread of fungi. I mist my tools with a dilute solution of hydrogen peroxide.

Always check the label when using fungicides and chemicals and follow any safety precautions.

Healthy habits: preventing problems before they start

The best way to deal with problems in bonsai is to stop them from happening in the first place. Having a consistent routine for your bonsai care will enable you to avoid most of the common issues faced by beginners.

Daily, seasonal and even annual habits are important when it comes to keeping your trees problem-free. These do not need to be complicated at all, just small tweaks and consistent actions to help keep your bonsai healthy and happy. Here is a checklist that you can come back to when you need to.

Healthy habits checklist

Water your trees when the soil begins to dry. Because I use free-draining soil, I water mine daily, even when it rains.

Fertilize your trees regularly, and according to the species and the season, so that they have the nutrients they need to stay strong.

Repot every two to five years depending on the species and age of the tree. Make sure your trees do not become too pot bound.

Weeds – pull them up as soon as they appear. They can take nutrients and water from your bonsai and may disturb the roots if left unchecked.

Check *nebari*. I use a nylon brush to scrub away any algae or moss growing on the *nebari* or at the base of the trunk.

Refresh the soil. If a full repot is not needed, refresh the top layer of soil each year to improve aeration and drainage, and to provide nutrients to the tree.

Wire checks are necessary to ensure that the wire is not biting in too much into the tree. If it is just starting to bite in, remove it right away to avoid scarring.

Pests and disease inspections should be carried out once a week. Look for fungal issues at the same time. Catching these early will prevent long-term damage.

Wound care – using cut putty on large cuts will protect wounds and encourage faster healing. In the growing season, you can reactivate the healing process by cutting into the callous tissue and reapplying cut putty.

Clear dead leaves to keep the soil surface clean. This will prevent fungal issues and maintain the tidiness of your trees.

Rotating the position of your trees once a week will ensure they get even light from all sides. This helps to keep growth balanced.

Maintenance pruning – removing any growth outside the bonsai profile – keeps a tree's shape and improves ramification. This is best done when your trees are actively growing.

Training assessment – taking time to analyse the development of your trees – is a task you can do once a month. For example, look to see whether any wire needs to be tweaked and check that your trees are developing the way you want them to.

Tool hygiene ensures your equipment is always clean and sharp. Wipe your tools with hydrogen peroxide between trees to disinfect them and avoid spreading disease. Sharpen them as needed – I do this once or twice a year.

Patience! The hardest but one of the best things you can do is simply to leave your trees alone. It may be tempting to do all the techniques that you have learned at once, but take it slow and put down the scissors from time to time to let your trees become strong.

Index

Acknowledgements & Credits

ACKNOWLEDGEMENTS

A special thanks to my family, especially my parents and my brother Sam, for their support and for helping me keep my online shop – www.notionbonsai.com – running while I was writing this book. I also want to thank my bonsai friends and the team of wonderful people from The Bright Press for their inspiration, encouragement and shared passion throughout this journey. Most of all, my deepest thanks go to my grandmothers, Gertie and Nell, who inspired my love of gardening when I was young and encouraged an interest that will stay with me forever.

To everyone who offered support, shared ideas or contributed helpful information along the way: Bjorn Bjorholm of Eisei-en Kyoto, Peter Chan of Herons Bonsai, Attila Csintalan of Fangorn Bonsai, Jelle Ferwerda of Bonsai Techniek, Mariusz Folda of IBUKI Bonsai, Phil Donnelly of Belfast Bonsai, Callan Jones of Rojin Bonsai Studio, Jay Madore and Nigel Saunders of The Bonsai Zone.

PICTURE CREDITS

Top= t Bottom= b Middle= m Right= r Left= l

Adam McCallion/17, 19-21, 30, 53, 54, 72, 73, 74, 75, 87, 92, 98, 100, 101, 102, 105 109, 111, 113, 114, 125, 127, 129, 131, 138, 139, 143, 145, 151, 152, 155, 159, 163. **Alamy**/Dorling Kindersley ltd: 18; Rodolfo Arpia: 32; Keith J Smith.: 50; victor cuenca lopez: 97; Dorling Kindersley ltd: 177. **Bjorn L Bjorholm www.bjornbjorholm.com @eiseienbonsai**/ 10,11, 34, 35, 38, 49, 60, 61, 90, 91, 140, 141. **Connor Cooper**/ 42. **Dreamstime**/ Nadimun Nahar: 78 b; Andra Maulana: 169; Walter Pall: 173. **Flickr**/Jerry Norbury: 16. **Freepic**/ 41 r. **Getty**/AaronLam: 6; Alvaro Medina Jurado: 23; CaroleGomez: 31; mtreasure: 37; Joel Rodgers: 41 l; Liudmila Chernetska: 70; krisanapong detraphiphat: 71; skaman306: 77; Nico De Pasquale Photography: 80; Douglas Sacha: 81 l; Nico De Pasquale Photography: 81 r; Boy_Anupong: 85 m; Alvaro Medina Jurado: 108; Carlo A: 115; Ollustrator: 133 tr; Steve Greaves:133 bl; Albert Fertl: 160; Elena Popova: 161 t; SimonSkafar: 161 b; OGphoto: 174. **Istock**/Heiko119: 16; jozefculak: 88. **Jonas Dupuich, Bonsai Tonight www.bonsaitonight.com @bonsaitonight**/131 b, 170, 177. **Shutterstock**/Renata Ty: 8-9; Food Impressions: 82-83; Oleggg: 85 t; MikalaiLipski: 85 m; Vanhouteen: 17; Versta: 65; sirirak kaewgorn: 78 mt; Oleggg: 87 r; AMJ Fotografia: 95; DrGB: 133 br; Byron Doyle-Zerbo: 171 l; Svetlana CA countryside:171 r; Svetlyachock: 184 t; Helga_foto: 184 m; Kazakov Maksim: 184 b; rdonar: 185 t; Amelia Martin: 185 m; Anne Webber: 185 b. **Unsplash**/Kari Shea: 12; Dan Crile: 78 mb; Csaba Talaber: 78 t; Csaba Talaber: 84; Milada Vigerova: 117; Raelle Gann-Owens (@raellego): 122, 123; Cecilia Nguyen: 168; WILDAN ABDILLAH: 177; Raelle Gann-Owens (@raellego):178, 179.